Co-operative Workplace Dispute Resolution

This book is lovingly dedicated to my father, William C. Hoffmann, and my mother, Mildred S. Hoffmann, who contributed to the success of this study in many small and large ways. I will always be grateful for their love, support, and confidence in me.

Co-operative Workplace Dispute Resolution

Organizational Structure, Ownership, and Ideology

ELIZABETH A. HOFFMANN

Purdue University, Indiana, USA

Routledge
Taylor & Francis Group

LONDON AND NEW YORK

First published 2012 by Gower Publishing

Published 2016 by Routledge
2 Park Square, Milton Park, Abingdon, Oxfordshire OX14 4RN
711 Third Avenue, New York, NY 10017, USA

First issued in paperback 2016

Routledge is an imprint of the Taylor & Francis Group, an informa business

Gower Applied Business Research
Our programme provides leaders, practitioners, scholars and researchers with thought provoking, cutting edge books that combine conceptual insights, interdisciplinary rigour and practical relevance in key areas of business and management.

British Library Cataloguing in Publication Data
Hoffmann, Elizabeth A.
  Co-operative workplace dispute resolution : organizational
  structure, ownership, and ideology.
  1. Producer cooperatives--Case studies. 2. Employee
  ownership--Case studies. 3. Labor disputes. 4. Mediation
  and conciliation, Industrial.
  I. Title
  338.6′9-dc23

Library of Congress Cataloging-in-Publication Data
Hoffmann, Elizabeth A.
  Co-operative workplace dispute resolution : organizational structure,
  ownership, and ideology / by Elizabeth A. Hoffmann.
    p. cm.
  Includes bibliographical references and index.
  ISBN 978-1-4094-2924-1 (hardback)
  1. Producer cooperatives. 2. Authority. 3. Industrial relations.
  I. Title.
  HD3121.H64 2011
  658.4′053--dc23

                                                                          2011052790

ISBN 13: 978-1-138-26873-9 (pbk)
ISBN 13: 978-1-4094-2924-1 (hbk)

Contents

List of Tables

List of Abbreviations

ADR   Alternative Dispute Resolution
ESOP   Employee Stock Ownership Plan
NUM   National Union of Mineworkers
TQM   Total Quality Management

Acknowledgements

I would like to begin by thanking my family and friends who have nurtured me—and this project—with constant support. I would like to specifically acknowledge several people. My parents, Bill and Milly Hoffmann, have cheered me on throughout my academic career and have always been a source of great love and inspiration. My husband, Rob Noll, has provided humor, love, and encouragement throughout all stages of this research—even traveling down a coal mine with me. Steven Hill and Kris Paap, through email or by phone, discussed my findings with me and offered me their invaluable perspectives. The Institute for Legal Studies' Fellows at the University of Wisconsin-Madison (UW-Madison) and the Lawrence University dissertators' group also provided helpful comments and feedback.

I especially wish to thank Professor Mark Suchman of Brown University. Throughout this project, Mark has offered excellent suggestions, profound feedback, and strategic advice. He has been an indispensable mentor in all aspects of my graduate career, offering continuous and enthusiastic support. Professor Lauren Edelman, of UC-Berkeley, was particularly instrumental in the early stages of this project, helping me craft my initial musings into coherent research questions. She continues to contribute much perceptive advice and support. Professor Jane Collins, of the University of Wisconsin, provided me with wonderful guidance and assistance in my many methodological questions and my various other queries. Professor Howard Erlanger, also of the University of Wisconsin, shared his profound insights on this project and extended continuous encouragement throughout this project and all my endeavors.

Great thanks are also due to the professors who worked with me during my time in the United Kingdom. Professor Richard Hyman, of the London School of Economics and Political Science, was a wonderful source of ideas and helped successfully launch the British data-gathering portion of this project.

Professor Davina Cooper, of the University of Kent, mentored me even before I arrived in the UK. Professor Joanna Liddle, of Warwick University, provided wonderful insights and many kindnesses; she even tracked down out-of-print materials that she knew would enrich my study.

Special thanks are also due to the many interviewees who participated in this study and to other people whom I did not interview, but who helped me make important contacts and gain entry into the businesses I studied, especially Norm Watson of the Welsh Co-operative Development Office. Many people also welcomed me into their homes, drove me to and from hotels, and facilitated contacts on my behalf.

I received funding from several sources that enabled me to conduct this research. To fund the transcription of several hundred hours of interviews, I received a National Science Foundation (NSF) Doctoral Dissertation Improvement Grant. A Small Grant Research Award from the UW-Madison Department of Sociology provided support for the initial pilot study. In order to collect the portion of my data in the United Kingdom, I received a University of Warwick-University of Wisconsin Doctoral Dissertation Grant. While in the United Kingdom, I also received a travel grant from the Warwick Business School to defer the costs of many trains and meals. I thank the funding agencies as well as the individuals who read my grant applications that enabled me to be awarded these grants.

About the Author

Elizabeth Hoffmann is an associate professor of Sociology at Purdue University, in West Lafayette, Indiana. She received her PhD and JD from the University of Wisconsin-Madison. Her interests in co-operative workplaces grew out of her interest in formal organizations and workplace dispute resolution. Dr Hoffmann continues her exploration of legal consciousness and dispute resolution in the workplace, her current scholarship continuing to bridge the areas of work-and-organizations and law-and-society: her research includes such topics as sexual harassment at work, the impact of loyalty on workplace disputes, lactating workers' rights mobilization, and how new laws are implemented in the workplace. The research presented in this book has won awards from the Industrial Relations Research Association, the Labor and Employment Relations Association, the Upjohn Institute for Employment Research, and the American Bar Foundation. Dr Hoffmann can be contacted by email at ehoffman@purdue.edu or by post at Department of Sociology, Purdue University, 351 Stone Hall, 700 W. State St., West Lafayette, IN 47907.

Introduction

Standing in the checkout line at a Home Depot recently, I overheard two middle-aged men waiting in line behind me talking about their work:

> *"Things would be different if I owned things," the first man said.*
>
> *"We make money for the company. We take the risks. We work like hell; we are the ones who know how things work," the second man added.*
>
> *"Or how things should work," the first man emphasized.*
>
> *"Those [management and ownership] guys, they don't know what we know, yet they make the decisions," said the second worker.*
>
> *The first man sighed. "Yeah, well. They own it. They make the decisions."*
>
> *"Hmph," the second man agreed. "Well, maybe we should be the ones owning it. Things would be different."*

Many employees have felt this way.

Yet only a few are able to embrace the possibility of becoming "the ones owning it."

This possibility—workers owning their own workplaces—is what this book explores. In most businesses, the majority of workers are employees. They earn wages or salaries. They might have the option to buy stocks, but other people own and run the company. In a worker co-operative, all employees own equal shares of the business and all owners work at the company. Often, worker co-operatives have radically flattened hierarchies—meaning they have fewer levels of management than most corporations.

These are substantial departures from the structures of conventional businesses. But do these differences actually change the workers' day-to-day experiences? Can being part of a worker co-operative ameliorate some of the worst aspects of people's jobs, such as their workplace disputes?

These are not easy questions to answer. In fact, most previous research on workplace disputes has relied exclusively on observations of traditional, hierarchical organizations. However, this book moves beyond observations to where no other study has gone: to consider how workers address formal and informal workplace disputes in the *absence* of formal hierarchy.

As the economy experiences occasional downturns as well as recessions—especially when a number of industries face financial crises—some companies will consider radical changes to the workplace. Both employees and managers have begun to question the usual ways of doing business. Worker-owned businesses may be part of the solution as people begin to re-evaluate how workplaces are organized.

At a theoretical level, this research is important because it helps to disentangle the impacts of hierarchy and power, while at an applied level it provides insights into the feasibility of a key plank in many progressive platforms: worker involvement and ownership. Specifically, this book compares employees' dispute resolution strategies at worker co-operatives and conventional businesses. Extant research suggests that organizational structure, ownership, and ideology greatly affect how employees address their problems at work (their grievance behavior) (e.g., Hochner et al. 1988; Hoffmann 2001; Rothschild and Whitt 1986; Tjosvold, Morishima, and Belsheim 1999; Tucker 1999; Whyte et al. 1983). This book draws on several literatures to address various predictions regarding dispute resolution in worker co-operatives. Some industrial relations literature cautions that worker co-operatives might not constitute viable alternatives to conventional, hierarchical businesses because worker co-operatives may be less efficient and less likely to succeed. However, other research has found that when co-operative businesses do struggle into existence and succeed, their workers enjoy greater respect and recognition and experience less labor-management conflict (e.g., Hochner et al. 1988). In fact, some literature on worker co-operatives suggests that evenly distributed power and greater worker participation produce workers who are able to assert their needs and raise necessary grievances. Research on grievance behavior asserts that worker co-operatives—where inclusion, equality and worker participation are officially encouraged—facilitate easier and more successful dispute resolution than other workplaces (e.g., Tjosvold, Morishima, and Belsheim 1999).

Worker co-operatives present a stark contrast to conventionally organized businesses in their efforts to evenly distribute power and encourage worker control through egalitarian ideologies and flattened management structures. Nevertheless, they share many goals of conventional businesses, such as producing profits and working efficiently. These similar goals allow for instructive comparisons.

This ground-breaking research compares dispute resolution strategies of members of co-operatives and employees of conventional companies in three industries: coal mining, taxicabs, and organic food distribution. Interestingly, the study did not reveal a worker co-operative impact *across* industries. For example, it did not find that all members of worker co-operatives resolved disputes more easily than employees of conventional businesses. However, the comparisons did reveal a worker co-operative effect *within* each industry. Specifically, the members of the worker co-operatives had more ways to resolve workplace disputes than their conventionally employed counterparts in the same industry.

To best understand how co-operatives work, this study does what none other has: it compares each co-operative to a matched conventional business within its industry. The chapters that follow compare each co-op with its conventional business counterpart, with specific focus on how the workers in each business address their workplace disputes. These contrasts offer concrete examples of the similarities and differences in dispute resolution behavior among employees in these two types of businesses. In this way, this book makes important strides in our understanding not only of worker co-operatives, but also of how dispute resolution options are managed and utilized in different circumstances. Both aspects of this book fill important gaps: examination of the factor of hierarchy in dispute resolution adds a completely new dimension to the somewhat stalled discussion of workplace disputes, while the focus on disputes allows for a fine degree of exploration into the contrasts between worker co-operatives and conventional businesses.

Chapter Summaries

In Chapter 1, "What Are Worker Co-operatives?" I detail what a worker co-operative is (a business owned and managed by its employees) and what it is not (an employee stock ownership plan [ESOP], a commune, etc.) This chapter explains why analysis of worker co-operatives is instructional beyond these relatively rare organizations. (According to the US Federation of Worker Co-operatives, the United States has about 300 worker co-operatives, employing more than 3,500 people. And according to *Co-operative Review*, published by the Union of Co-operative Enterprises in Britain, 4,820 co-operatives provide 205,800 jobs in that country.) As businesses that practice an extreme form of shared organizational power, worker co-operatives fully embrace what many organizations currently adopt partially in the form of quality circles, total quality management, shared governance, and other programs that share managerial power in limited ways with employees. As the logical conclusion of such employee-empowerment innovations, an analysis of worker co-operatives is useful on many levels. This chapter also analyzes current research and debates regarding the efficiency and sustainability of worker co-operatives.

Chapter 2, "What is Workplace Dispute Resolution," examines what workplace disputes are and why they are both difficult and important to study. Many disciplines—law, sociology, political science, management and human relations, anthropology, and more—investigate dispute resolution. Disputes exist in nearly all facets of life, and the way disputes are resolved in a workplace provides important insights about the organization and how power is negotiated within it. Because workplace disputes are often considered the worst aspect of people's jobs (and inspire them most to want to change jobs or workplaces), this book assesses whether members of co-operatives fare any better than employees of conventional businesses when it comes to resolving conflict at work.

Chapter 3, "Three Different Worker Co-operatives," introduces the reader to the co-operatives I studied, situating their industries, their physical locations, the composition of their workforces, and their ideological perspectives. Each worker co-operative is in a different industry—coal, taxicab driving, and whole food distribution—and each came into being in a different way. Coal Co-operative (I've used pseudonyms in all cases) formed when a British coal mine was targeted for closing and the soon-to-be out-of-work miners bought it themselves. Cab drivers in a medium-sized Midwestern city in the United States formed Co-op Cab while striking against a private company. And in the 1970s, a handful of current and former college students formed a small organic food co-operative in northern England, which gradually grew into a substantial organization (Organix Co-op). This chapter also introduces the three conventional, hierarchically organized businesses in each industry which serve as comparisons to the co-operatives. These businesses are similar in terms of size as well as sharing comparable gender and racial compositions and approximate organizational ages. Chapters 4 through 6 examine dispute resolution at each worker co-operative.

In Chapter 4, "Mining the Depths of Co-ownership: The Coal Industry," I explore how at Coal Co-operative the workers' attitudes toward disputes were greatly influenced by the mining industry's militant history, the absence of other "quality men's jobs" in the area, and the local mining tradition. These factors made the coal industry unique from the other two in that miners in neither mine considered quitting as a way to resolve workplace disputes.

Chapter 5, "Legal Consciousness on the Road: The Taxicab Industry," compares working conditions for workers in the taxicab industry in a Midwestern city. Interviews of drivers revealed that employees at Private Taxi, the conventional company, rarely expected to resolve disputes at all, and they only used informal means when they did. In contrast, members of the taxicab co-operative regularly resolved disputes both formally and informally, with women more often using formal channels and men taking advantage of informal connections to resolve disputes.

In Chapter 6, "Loyalty Instead of Leaving: Dispute Resolution in the Organics Industry," the research revealed that workers at Organix, the co-operative company, were able to resolve disputes through both formal and informal means. While these workers were quite loyal to their co-operative, a high percentage of them said they would leave the company if they came into ideological conflict with the co-operative. In contrast, employees at HealthBite, the conventional company, rarely tried to resolve their disputes at all. Most often, they relied on toleration strategies, and when they did attempt dispute resolution, they worked informally. At Organix Co-op, class divisions became more prominent after the co-operative moved from a university town to a depressed industrial area. Here, less-educated, working-class members found informal dispute resolution difficult and relied exclusively on formal routes.

Some co-operatives struggled in their efforts to achieve the co-operative ideal of equality at work. The difficulties that Co-op Cab and Organix Co-op had are discussed in Chapter 7, "Co-operative Struggles: Struggles Toward the Goal of Equality." Despite these co-operatives' commitment and hard work to create more egalitarian workplaces, some of their members enjoyed "insider" status and heightened power in the workplace. One of the most important benefits of this inside status was the ability to address grievances informally or formally, while their co-workers could only rely on the formal grievance resolutions procedures.

Chapter 8, "Lessons for the Rest of Us: The Co-operative Landscape," compares the dispute resolution strategies at each co-operative with those in the matched conventional, hierarchical business. This study did not find, as some earlier scholarship predicted, two different modes of dispute resolution: one for co-operatives and one for hierarchical companies. Yet, even though the co-operative workers across all three industries did not approach disputes identically, a clear pattern emerged: the workers in the co-operatives had more methods for resolving their disputes than their counterparts in conventional businesses. Finally, realizing that few businesses will change themselves into worker co-operatives, this chapter offers suggestions for mainstream businesses.

This is the first book to speak to activists, business leaders, and rank-and-file workers about this long-awaited topic. Although the extant literature in recent years has shifted its focus away from dispute resolution, how problems are handled is a key element of the quality of work life and is of great importance to workers and managers alike. This book's particular examination of dispute resolution strategies contributes a rich discussion of how hierarchy—or the flattening of it—might affect workplace dispute resolution.

This is a hopeful book. It examines an innovation in workplace organization—worker co-operatives—and presents the possibility for improving working conditions in a variety of industries. Even though most businesses would never consider completely restructuring themselves to become worker co-operatives, some aspects of the employee ownership and involvement can often be available to workers at more conventional businesses as well.

Works Cited

Hochner, A., Granrose, C.S., Goode, J., Simon, E. and Appelbaum, E. (1988). *Worker Buyouts and QWL*: W. E. Upjohn Institute for Employment Research.

Hoffmann, E.A. (2001). Confrontations and Compromise: Dispute Resolution at a Worker Co-operative Coal Mine. *Law & Social Inquiry* 26:555–596.

Rothschild, J. and Whitt, J.A. (1986). *The Co-operative Workplace: Potentials and Dilemmas of Organizational Democracy and Participation*. Cambridge: Cambridge University Press.

Tjosvold, D., Morishima, M. and Belsheim, J.A. (1999). Complaint Handling on the Shop Floor: Co-operative Relationships and Open-Minded Strategies. *The International Journal of Conflict Management* 10:45–68.

Tucker, J. (1999). *The Therapeutic Corporation*. New York: Oxford University Press.

Whyte, W.F., Hammer, T.H., Meek, C.B., Nelson, R. and Stern, R.N. (1983). *Worker Participation and Ownership*. Ithica, N.Y.: ILR Press.

1
What Are Worker Co-operatives?

Worker co-operatives are organizations with equally shared worker ownership and egalitarian ideologies. As "[t]he oldest vision for an emancipatory alternative to capitalism," according to Wright (2010: 165), worker co-operatives present an almost instinctive reaction to the alienation of workers that capitalism created because worker co-operatives reverse that separation of the worker from the means of production. Worker co-operative organizational structures are flattened, with minimal hierarchical levels of supervision, or no formal hierarchies at all: they exist in a wide variety of workplaces—bakeries, lumberyards, coal mines, theaters, grocery stores, and bicycle repair shops— but are less familiar to most people than consumer co-operatives, in which shoppers buy into an organization to receive discounts on future purchases.

The existence of worker co-operatives tests a number of beliefs strongly held by scholars and non-scholars for many years. Academics and the general public often assume that as the size of an organization increases, the need for more layers of management increases. Because of this widely held belief, much research on organizations focuses on the importance of hierarchy, and there has been little exploration into alternative organizations. Yet, knowledge of co-operatively run organizations can lead to a greater understanding of all organizations, which may be radically affected by the level of hierarchy present. It is also important to understand what alternatives exist to mainstream, conventional models of organization. To understand the challenge presented by worker co-operatives, we will examine what other researchers have written about how organizations work and what others can teach us about co-operatives.

The Assumption of Hierarchy

Conventional businesses are organized hierarchically, with top-down decision-making and with information generally flowing up to management: in this arrangement, workers lack control over their conditions at work and only highly filtered information reaches the rank-and-file. Managerial decisions are made in upper levels of the hierarchy, and those decisions are not necessarily based on local knowledge or diverse expertise (Bailyn 1997). Yet, despite these drawbacks, some scholars have argued that hierarchical bureaucracy is the natural order of things, and will come to dominate nearly all aspects of life. These scholars further argue that once it is established, bureaucracy becomes firmly entrenched and is the most difficult type of social structure to destroy. Max Weber, for example, stated that "[t]he ruled, for their part, cannot dispense with or replace the bureaucratic apparatus of authority once it exists" (Weber 1946: 26). Indeed, we encounter bureaucracy in almost every aspect of our lives.

According to a number of scholars, the operation of an organization without a hierarchy would be "utopian" and impossible to achieve in modern society (Weber 1946: 27). Moreover, scholars like Weber reason that the absence of hierarchy is impracticable because of hierarchy's strong link to bureaucracy; a link that he holds is inevitable in modern society. Hierarchy provides both the apparatus that bureaucracy needs and the foundation of beliefs on which bureaucracy bases its claims. Weber (1946) argues that the legitimization of bureaucracy requires the belief hierarchy perpetuates: that bureaucracy should be followed for the sake of efficiency. Without efficiency as a highly prioritized goal, bureaucracy appears less essential, since a key advantage of bureaucracies is their more efficient operation of administrative functions (Ouchi 1980).

Like Weber, Robert Michels shares reservations about large-scale, non-hierarchical organizations (Michels 1962: 38, 43). His classic statement, "Who says organization, says oligarchy," vehemently expresses this disbelief in the possibility of successful collective management (Michels 1962: 49). Arguing more strongly than Weber for a natural inclination toward hierarchy, he states, "organization implies the tendency to oligarchy ... As a result of organization, every party or professional union becomes divided into a minority of directors and a majority of directed" (Michels 1962: 42).

Michels holds that an organization must have strong leaders. According to his line of reasoning, the masses choose leaders, who in time become the rulers of the people who selected them. In this regard, a system of domination is inevitably created, whether or not a democratic base or an ideological commitment to equality exist. Importantly, once the power is transferred, it remains in the hands of those few individuals (Michels 1962: 49).

This transfer of power from workers to a hierarchy of managers is not only inevitable but also universal, according to Michels. "The formation of oligarchies within the various forms of democracy is the outcome of organic necessity, and consequently affects every organization, be it socialist or even anarchist," he writes (Michels 1962: 50). Thus, despite commitment by members to ideologies that seek to redistribute power throughout the masses, power will be transferred, accumulating in only a small subgroup. Hierarchy, then, emerges as the outcome of technical conditions (Michels 1962: 44). Michels argues that an unequal distribution of power is inevitable and that this mandates a hierarchical arrangement to utilize this power. In addition, as the division of labor becomes greater, hierarchy becomes more complicated. The larger and more complicated an organization becomes, the more hierarchy becomes unavoidable. This point illustrates a theoretical difference between Weber and Michels. Michels believes that, as an organization grows, technical conditions necessitate hierarchy, while Weber argues that technical conditions only make hierarchy more desirable, not necessarily inevitable, because hierarchy allows an organization to deal most effectively with increased technical complications.

Because most organizational theorists assume Michels' "Iron Law of Oligarchy" as a given, few researchers have sought to explore the functioning of organizations that challenge the notion of the inevitability of hierarchy and oligarchy. Several studies that examine hierarchy conclude that hierarchy is unavoidable. In their 1956 study of a democratic labor union, the International Typographers Union, Lipset, Trow, and Coleman, argue that hierarchy is necessary and inevitable in larger organizations: they conclude that the structure of large-scale organizations "inherently requires the development of bureaucratic patterns" (Lipset, Trow, and Coleman 1956: 361). They find that the conditions necessary for the institutionalization of bureaucracy and democracy are incompatible (Lipset, Trow, and Coleman 1956).

Even writers in the popular press have raised the question of the inevitability of hierarchical businesses, and found an answer similar to Michels' Iron Law. For example, in a much noted *Forbes* article, Peter Drucker writes, "[O]ne hears a great deal today about 'the end of hierarchy.' This is blatant nonsense. In any institution, there has to be a final authority, that is, a 'boss'—someone who can make the final decision and who can then expect to be obeyed" (Drucker October 5, 1998: 158).

In other research, scholars assert that hierarchy is not just inevitable, but beneficial. Hannan and Freeman suggest that the likelihood of success is diminished if an organization operates without a hierarchical structure, although they, too, do not identify hierarchy specifically. First, they argue that the possibility of structural innovations may cause a loss of technical efficiency (Meyer and Rowan 1977) because implementing a new or alternative way to operate may harm the actual functioning of the organization, making survival less likely (Hannan and Freeman 1989). They further argue that such structural innovations may create costs in legitimacy for the organization with regard to its institutional environment. Organizations are more likely to fail when they deviate from the prescriptions of institutionalizing myths (Hannan and Freeman 1989).

Institutionalist theorists argue that hierarchy is an important rational myth. According to this line of reasoning, if an organization operates without the structure of hierarchy, it may lose the legitimacy it needs to succeed. The institutional legitimacy of hierarchy makes social action more easily reproduced (Zucker 1977). However, institutional theorists do not agree with Weber and others on the technical benefits of hierarchy.

In contrast, other scholars do not perceive a degree of hierarchy as beneficial. Some classical theorists have perceived hierarchy negatively, the most famous of these being Marx. Understanding organizations as power systems that are designed to maximize profit and control, Marx argued that hierarchy is utilized to "deskill" workers, rather than to improve efficiency. Thus, hierarchy is not a rational system of co-ordination, as Weber believed, but "an instrument of control and a means of accumulating capital through the appropriation of surplus value" (Scott 1992: 115).

Although Marxists assert that hierarchy is used in the workplace to control and oppress, they do not necessarily support systems of collective management. Marxists argue that co-operative management is misguided because it fails to challenge the fundamental exploitative nature of organizations. Marx himself felt that co-operatively held property would precede socialism. However, the type of social property arrangement he proposed would be formally developed on a national scale and sponsored by government (Marx and Engels 1986). Wright explains that Marx initially rejected worker co-operatives, although later in his life Marx concluded that worker co-operatives were "a legitimate element of socialist strategy" (Wright 2010: 165). Rothschild and Whitt (1986) argue that though many members of worker co-operatives would label themselves as Marxists and subscribe to Marxist ideals and critiques of capitalism, their community-level agendas and their beliefs in the importance of grassroots movements are not supported by Marx.

Organizations Without Hierarchy

Despite these assertions by a range of scholars, collectively run organizations attempt to escape from the inevitabilities of hierarchical administration. Many members of worker co-operatives strive to create entities that exist without one person or a small, select group holding the ultimate authority (Rothschild and Whitt 1986: 52). Some contemporary theorists suggest that hierarchy, which would inevitably be produced in most situations, is not inevitable in less conventional, alternative groups. These researchers argue that, because these subgroups interpret conditions differently from mainstream society, "hierarchy-related" conditions may not necessarily lead to hierarchy for them.

Collins and other scholars have argued that certain subgroups within society differ in their orientations toward assumed, "taken-for-granted" norms and in how they invest cultural resources (Collins 1981). People who hold less conventional beliefs, therefore, may not assume that hierarchy is inevitable. In addition, Scott (1992) has argued that cultural frames establish which means are appropriate and which ends are desirable. Ethnic subpopulations, such as the Basque in Spain, present the classic example of a homogenous subgroup which created a large, successful co-operative (Wright 2010). In this way, people with cultural frames that differ from those of mainstream society may view means and ends that are commonly deemed utopian—such as non-hierarchical workplaces—as highly possible and worthwhile. In their work on various forms of co-operatives, Rothschild and Whitt (1986) found that interviewees often held non-conventional beliefs, especially with regard to hierarchy and efficiency, the capitalist economic system, and government actions. Many people in their study identified themselves as Marxists or anarchists, or aligned themselves with such ideologies. These ideologies encourage values that contrast and oppose those of mainstream society.

Powell and DiMaggio (1991: 29) argue that institutional models will not be imported in their entirety into systems that are very different from the ones in which they originate. They note that despite these subgroups' alternative ideologies and commitment to eliminating certain aspects of conventional organizations, they will nevertheless continue to operate using some elements of the system they oppose. Thus, these subgroups may retain some aspects of mainstream organizational culture, such as paychecks, regular operating or business hours, and income-tax deductions, while not necessarily including all aspects, namely hierarchy.

Scott argues that, under some conditions, institutional environments may reduce rather than increase the quantity or elaborateness of organizational structure. He explains that cultural controls can substitute for structural controls in some circumstances: "When beliefs are widely shared and categories and procedures are taken for granted, it is less essential that they be formally encoded in organizational structures." (Scott 1987: 507). This argument suggests that when the members of an organization share goals, the structures of the organization can be less rigid. This condition allows for the possibility of operating without needing a hierarchy to impose elaborate structure and control on the members of the organization.

The lack of need for hierarchy may be more likely in organizations where members not only share goals, but also share more subtle cultural understandings and symbols that provide order. Thus, writes Scott, "(o)rganizational structures may only be required to support and supplement those cultural systems that exercise a direct influence on participants" (Scott 1987: 507). This argument suggests that organizations with a high level of homogeneity—where goals, beliefs, conceptual language, and symbols are shared among the members—can avoid the creation of hierarchy.

Ouchi identified a type of organization that tends to be less hierarchical, the "clan" (Ouchi 1980). According to Ouchi's model, economic relationships depend first on whether the parties all share the same goals or must be induced (such as by a paycheck) to work toward someone else's goal, and whether the exact tasks each person must perform are consistent and clear, or are ambiguous and need to be continuously articulated—"performance ambiguity." Ouchi asserts that there are three different ways of organizing economic relationships based on these two factors: (1) markets when the actors do not share the same objectives or goals, yet there is no ambiguity as to what each actor will do to fulfill his or her part of the bargain; (2) bureaucracies when there are high levels of both goal incongruence and performance ambiguity; and (3) clans where goals are shared among actors even though performance ambiguity remains high. Ouchi's model shows that markets, whose actors hold different (even opposing) goals, rely on the immediacy of transactions to ensure compliance and performance, while bureaucracies, whose actors also lack similar goals, use the authority of hierarchy and rules to ensure long-range compliance. Clans rely on socialization to achieve these same goals, which then regulate behavior and enforce boundaries as the specifics of each party's performance develops (Ouchi 1980).

Like a bureaucracy, a clan orchestrates long-term performance. However, rather than addressing differences between the employers' goals and the workers' goals by maximizing power imbalances and supervision, clans create goal congruence among workers and employers, whether by carefully selecting new members or through socialization. The clan develops an organic solidarity among all members of the organization. This high level of goal congruence removes the need for a hierarchy of power and supervision, since "[w]here individual and organizational interests overlap ... rewards can be achieved at a relatively low transaction cost," writes Ouchi (1980:136). In this way, clans do not have to rely on Weber's rational legal form, but instead call on the "[c]ommon values and beliefs [that] provide the harmony of interest" for the organization (Ouchi 1980:136). Thus, the clan form eliminates goal incongruence by exerting informal power to teach common values, removing the need for hierarchy.

While Ouchi and his collaborators primarily focused on clans operating in modern, mainstream industrial organizations, his concept of the clan can also be applied to the worker co-operative. Ouchi used his clan concept to briefly discuss the business side of the utopian communities Kanter researched. He compared his explanation of the workings of clans with Kanter's discussion of the co-operative communities she studied. Kanter found that a key to a collective's success was a widely shared belief that individual interests are best served when they are immersed into the interests of the greater whole (Kanter 1972).

The importance of shared goals and beliefs that run counter to those of mainstream society has been supported by the findings of Collins (1981) and Zucker (1977). Additionally, Swidler's work on "free schools"—schools that attempted to minimize the level of authority, hierarchy, and power differences in the classroom—demonstrates that the perpetuation of a "common purpose" is essential for ideological appeals to be effective (Swidler 1979). Rothschild and

Whitt, in their work on a variety of collectivist organizations, also emphasize the necessity of ideological appeals as the main means of control in order to avoid need for a centralized, hierarchical authority (Rothschild and Whitt 1986).

None of this previous research, however, has focused on dispute resolution. For example, while both Kanter's work on communes (1972) and Swidler's research on free schools (1979) provide in-depth analyses of non-hierarchical institutions, neither study examines co-operative workplaces or examines dispute resolution in any kind of depth. Rothschild and Whitt (1986), Iannello (1992) and Hacker (1989) do examine worker co-operatives, but do not explore dispute resolution in depth.

These studies of collectively run organizations have found that the absence of hierarchy alters more than just organizational structure. Interpersonal dynamics, the languages of power and authority, and available means and procedures are all affected by the elimination of hierarchy in an organization (Kanter 1972; Rothschild and Whitt 1986; Swidler 1979). Thus, it is important to study non-hierarchical as well as hierarchical organizations.

Management Trends

Worker co-operatives are extreme examples of businesses where the concepts of flattened workplace hierarchies, shared ownership, and collective management are put into practice. While few managers would consider converting their businesses to co-operatives, some current management trends incorporate certain aspects of worker co-operatives. A number of corporations speak of moving toward greater worker participation in managerial-type decisions and greater sharing of information (Heckscher 1997). Yet, management often fails to implement reforms initially celebrated by the company, particularly by those at the top. The hurdle to such implementation is not unwillingness from workers, but resistance from management, especially from those at the level of first-line supervisor. Milkman (1997) emphasizes that what is striking is not that workers pose no resistance to management's reforms, presented as necessary to ensure or improve the company's competitiveness, but rather that the workers are actually enthusiastic about these changes. Milkman explains that workers, such as the assembly line workers at GM that she studied, so disliked the conventional system of management that they willingly bought into a promise of any new type of management (Milkman 1997).

In fact, many workers are dissatisfied with the way management treats them. Comps and Savoie (1977: 18) assert that "fully half of America's workers report they do not get the respect and recognition they deserve from their organizations." Workers across the public, private, and non-profit sectors, in both union and non-union workplaces and from entry-level manual positions to top professional levels expressed these sentiments. The importance of being treated respectfully has been well established by both scholarly research and popular understandings. However, most employees do not prize the tangible awards commonly doled out by managers seeking to increase the level of employee recognition (certificates, monthly awards, and special dinners). Rather, Comps and Savoie (1977) found that employees most appreciate *interpersonal* respect and recognition.

A number of human resource practices attempt to improve the interpersonal respect and recognition given to employees. Quality-of-work-life and employee-involvement programs are some of the earliest types of direct employee participation initiatives to gain widespread attention in the early 1980s (Tjosvold, Morishima, and Belsheim 1999). Other programs include high-performance work systems, and employee stock option plans (ESOPs). These innovations reflect some—although clearly not all—of the goals of worker co-operatives. They also affect the bottom line. High-performance work systems are often characterized by incentive pay, increased teamwork, employment security guarantees, flexible job assignments, off-line training, and information sharing with rank-and-file workers. Researchers have found that these human resource practices encourage better worker performance (Ichniowski, Kochan, and Olson 1998). Blasi (1988) found that employee stock ownership has positive effects on profitability, productivity, and compensation. In addition, Tjosvold et al. assert that ESOPs and other employee profit-sharing plans as well as quality-of-work-life programs may reduce grievances (Tjosvold, Morishima, and Belsheim 1999).

Mackin (1997) looks specifically at the effect of employee ownership on productivity, performance, and worker commitment. In his study of businesses with participatory management (some employee-owned and others with conventional ownership), he reports that the businesses with participatory practices alone did not see the sales and employment benefits enjoyed by the firms that had employee ownership as well as participatory management. While earlier researchers had observed that participatory work organizations created "a psychological 'sense of ownership'" among employees, Mackin found that this "sense of ownership" was insufficient to produce the level of worker buy-in that actual employee ownership produced. He argues that workers "are able to make a critical distinction between 'psychological' and 'real' ownership and, controlling for other variables, will hold out their highest performance for workplaces which traffic in the real thing" (Mackin 1997: 68).

Similarly, Russell's work confirms the importance of shared ownership over shared management practices alone. He found that businesses with more co-operative management did not have more positive worker experiences, more pro-worker management agendas, or lower amounts of labor-management conflict than those with conventional management. He examined two types of management: "Fordist," with a "matrix of rigid and bureaucratically defined job classifications and series of repetitive physical motions directed by others," and "post-Fordist," in which the worker is a "member of a self-directed, problem-solving team" with broad responsibilities, job rotation, multi-skilling, "pay-for-knowledge," and profit-sharing schemes (Russell 1999: 199). In the post-Fordist businesses, the restructuring did not lead to the elimination of labor-management conflict, but only changed the lines of conflict to the issue of job security (Russell 1999). His comparative study found that managerial agendas and workers' experiences are substantially similar at Fordist and post-Fordist companies. The post-Fordist concepts of job rotation, job reassignment, and job expansion were widespread at all four worksites as well. At all worksites he found workers taking on more job duties without any simultaneous increases in their work becoming more fulfilling or interesting. He also found that all the "restructuring strategies" meant work intensification and employment reduction; they were really serving to get workers to do "more with less for less" (Russell 1999: 199).

This literature on organizations implies that if worker co-operatives are to create a viable alternative to conventional, hierarchical businesses, they might have a precarious existence. These co-operative organizations may be less efficient and less likely to succeed. However, if they do struggle into existence, their workers might enjoy many benefits, including greater respect and recognition, higher efficiency, and less labor-management conflict.

Worker Co-operatives: Ideals and Reality

According to the generally accepted ideology of worker co-operatives, many of the barriers to workers asserting their concerns and raising their voices, as discussed in the next chapter, should be greatly reduced—if not altogether vanquished—in a worker co-op (Thornley 1981; Wright 2010). Because all the workers are owners, they should be empowered to assert their needs and express their feelings and frustrations without fear. The co-operative structure and ideology should enable members to raise issues, concerns, and problems, even unpopular ones. All are equal, and everyone has an equal chance to be heard.

In addition, co-operatives should help to eliminate the constraints of gender norms and double standards and make efforts to assist members to move away from society's prescribed roles (Cornforth et al. 1988). The experience of being a member of a worker co-operative should strengthen one's ability to pursue wrongful actions and provide the confidence and empowerment necessary to raise a grievance over unjust treatment. Linehan and Tucker (1983: 18) argue that "(b)y participating in co-operatives, workers acquire new skills in organization and in self-management. Together they achieve what none of them could do alone. In this way, workers' co-operation allows people an opportunity to gain self-confidence and become more self-reliant." The reduced reliance on control in worker co-operatives allows for greater worker initiative and for team co-operation in problem-solving, in contrast to top-down monitoring and highly filtered employee information (Putterman 1982: 147). However, the extent to which co-operative ideology is realized in the day-to-day operations of worker co-operatives is controversial.

Several varieties of co-operatives exist today, of which a "worker co-operative" is only one. The fundamental principle underlying a worker co-operative is that control of the business is gained by investing one's labor in it. As stated earlier, this fact differentiates worker co-ops from consumer or agricultural-producer co-operatives where authority is derived from patronage or a shareholding in the ownership of the enterprise (Linehan and Tucker 1983). However, worker co-operatives were often begun as producer or consumer co-ops, designed to produce a product that the group specifically needed (Voorhis 1961). Compared to mainstream equivalent businesses, advocates say, worker co-operatives can run more productively and can generate more jobs from the same level of capital investment (Jackall and Levin 1984). Furthermore, since the workers, as the owners, determine how the work is to be conducted, all work can be organized according to the preference of the members of the co-operatives, thereby increasing job satisfaction (Jackall and Levin 1984).

However, commitment to co-operative management and ownership must be matched with a similar commitment to being a stable business (Cowling

1943; Rock 1991). This delicate balance is often difficult to achieve. Unlike conventional businesses, which view their services and products merely as essentials of the profit-making process rather than as ends in themselves, worker co-operatives produce goods and services to benefit those who use them as well as those who produce them (Wright 2010). For this reason, many production worker co-operatives have refused to make goods that are not ecologically sound or are war-related (Linehan and Tucker 1983). Market pressures can exacerbate tensions between a co-operative's goals of self-management and the need to survive economically in a competitive economy: in addition, being a member of a worker co-operative places great time demands on individuals beyond their working hours. The hours required for committee meetings, self-education, and decision-making place additional burdens on workers' time. Such a demanding lifestyle, especially burdensome when the co-op is newly formed, can severely dampen the appeal of the non-hierarchical workplace (Linehan and Tucker 1983).

Co-operative Management and Supervision

The tension between owners/managers and workers is well recognized in conventionally owned and hierarchically run businesses. Workers are motivated to minimize their labor, while owners are motivated to minimize wages. Putterman asserts that a worker-owner in a worker co-operative is still motivated to minimize his own labor, but wants to maximize the labor of his fellow workers. In contrast, in a conventional business, any difference of labor greater than wages between fellow workers goes only to the owners, and workers have little interest in the rate of their co-workers' work. This leads to different control possibilities facing the two types of businesses, which could result in different organizational characteristics (Putterman 1982). Putterman argues the following:

> An ideal organizational structure, in this case, would be an entrepreneurial firm which is small enough so that the owner-manager can monitor the work performance of all participants. It has been argued that the monitoring of all other participants by the owner-manager of this type of firm will be more efficient than a symmetrical system of mutual monitoring in a worker-run enterprise, because all benefits of monitoring flow to the owner-manager in the first case, whereas the benefits of monitoring might be so diluted among the members of a labor-managed firm that the individual incentive to monitor fellow workers is quite small. (1982: 145)

In worker co-operatives, according to Putterman, worker-*managers* have no increased incentive to closely monitor other members, since, unlike capitalist owners of private companies, they cannot claim any residual revenue created by some workers' greater efforts. However, other workers have greater incentive to monitor each other, with possible mutual monitoring increasing effort and incomes of all members. Putterman asserts that this effect will be greater in small workplaces, where even one individual's increased labor has a greater impact on the group. Thus, co-operatives will be characterized by greater peer control and less supervisory control than conventional businesses.

Other researchers agree that the shared ownership of co-operatives provides strong personal incentives both for co-workers to pressure each other to work hard and for self-monitoring individuals to be productive. Thus, the extent of supervision necessary is often greatly lessened, if not eliminated in worker co-operatives (Jackall and Levin 1984). In addition, members have both the opportunity as workers—and the incentive as owners—to acquire detailed information about the effectiveness of the current mode of working within the company. This allows for the most effective management since there is, at least potentially, no gap in knowledge between management decisions and the "front line" experiences of the workers (Hansmann 1990).

Because most workers have never experienced self-management and have few models that co-operative members can emulate, workers in co-operatives may feel that they need or want conventional supervisory management. As a result, workers may try to re-interpret the co-operatives' worker-managers as conventional hierarchical managers. This may mean that these managers are accorded inappropriate deference or disproportionate scorn, merely because of their perceived association with conventional managers (Linehan and Tucker 1983). Workers may hold ideological positions that equate management with capitalist oppression or they may have a history of being antagonized by management at previous jobs (Cornforth et al. 1988). Putterman argues that, because of the start-up costs and steep learning curves, "we could expect only groups of workers who view hierarchical capitalism as particularly odious, or those trying to save their jobs in failing capitalist firms, to be prepared to commit themselves to worker-run enterprises" (Putterman 1982: 151).

Assuming workers do commit themselves to membership in a non-hierarchical business, what difference will this structure have on their abilities to address problems and conflicts in the workplace? I turn next to literature on dispute resolution to examine how people address conflicts when problems arise at work, and the power dynamics that might be avoidable in worker co-operatives.

Works Cited

Bailyn, L. (1997). Transforming Work: How Do We Live With It? *Perspectives on Work* 1:10–13.

Blasi, J.R. (1988). *Employee Ownership: Revolution or Rip-off?* New York: Ballinger.

Collins, R. (1981). On the Micro-Foundations of Macro-Sociology. *American Journal of Sociology* 86:984–1014.

Comps, J.J. and Savoie, E.J. (1977). The Basic Workplace Promise: Respect and Recognition. *Perspectives on Work* 1.

Cornforth, C., Thomas, A., Lewis, J. and Spear, R. (1988). *Developing Successful Worker Co-operatives*. London: Sage Publications.

Cowling, E. (1943). *Co-operatives in America: Their Past, Present and Future*. New York: Coward-McCann, Inc.

Drucker, P.F. (October 5, 1998). Management's New Paradigms. *Forbes*, 152–177.

Hacker, S. (1989). *Pleasure, Power, and Technology: Some Tales of Gender Engineering and the Co-operative Workplace*. Boston: Unwin Hyman.

Hannan, M.T. and Freeman, J. (1989). *Organizational Ecology*. Cambridge: Harvard University Press.

Hansmann, H. (1990). When Does Worker Ownership Work? ESOPs, Law Firms, Codetermination, and Economic Democracy. *Yale Law Journal* 99:1749–1816.

Heckscher, C. (1997). The Changing Social Contract for White-Collar Workers. *Perspectives on Work* 1:18–21.

Iannello, K.P. (1992). *Decisions Without Authority: Feminist Interventions in Organization Theory and Practice*. New York: Routlege.

Ichniowski, C., Kochan, T.A. and Olson, C.A. (1998). Assessing the Effects of HR on Firms, Individuals, and Society: The Role of the HR Network. *Perspectives on Work* 2.

Jackall, R. and Levin, H.M. (1984). *Worker Co-operatives in America*. Berkeley: University of California Press.

Kanter, R.M. (1972). *Commitment and Community*. Cambridge: Harvard University Press.

Linehan, M. and Tucker, V. (1983). *Workers' Co-operatives: Potential and Problems*. Midleton, County Cork, Ireland: Litho Press Co.

Lipset, S.M., Trow, M.A. and Coleman, J.S. (1956). *Union Democracy*. New York: Free Press.

Mackin, C. (1997). Employee Ownership and Industrial Relations. *Perspectives on Work* 1.

Marx, K. and Engels, F. (1986). *Selected Works: their Essential Thinking in Philosophy, Political Science, History, Social Change and Communism.* New York: International Publishers.

Meyer, J.W. and Rowan, B. (1977). Institutionalized Organizations: Formal Structure as Myth and Ceremony. *American Journal of Sociology* 83:340–363.

Michels, R. (1962). *Political Parties*. Translated by E. Paul and C. Paul. New York: The Crowell-Collier Publishing Company.

Milkman, R. (1997). *Farewell to the Factory: Auto Workers in the Late Twentieth Century*. Berkeley: University of California Press.

Ouchi, W.G. (1980). Markets, Bureaucracies, and Clans. *Administrative Science Quarterly* 25.

Powell, W.W. and DiMaggio, P.J. (1991). *The New Institutionalism in Organizational Analysis*. Chicago: The University of Chicago Press.

Putterman, L. (1982). Some Behavioral Perspectives on the Dominance of Hierarchical Over Democratic Forms of Enterprise. *Journal of Economic Behavior and Organization* 3:139–160.

Rock, C. (1991). Workplace Democracy in the United States. pp. 37–58 in *Worker Empowerment: the Struggle for Workplace Democracy*, edited by J.D. Wisman. New York: The Bootstrap Press.

Rothschild, J. and Whitt, J.A. (1986). *The Co-operative Workplace: Potentials and Dilemmas of Organizational Democracy and Participation*. Cambridge: Cambridge University Press.

Russell, B. (1999). *More with Less: Work Reorganization in the Canadian Mining Industry*. Toronto: University of Toronto Press.

Scott, W.R. (1987). The Adolescence of Institutional Theory. *Administrative Science Quarterly* 32.

Scott, W.R. (1992). *Organizations: Rational, Natural and Open Systems*. Englewood Cliffs, New Jersey: Prentice Hall.

Swidler, A. (1979). *Organizations Without Authority: Dilemmas of Social Control in Free Schools*. Cambridge, Mass: Harvard University.

Thornley, J. (1981). *Workers' Co-operatives: Jobs and Dreams*. London: Heinemann Educational Books.

Tjosvold, D., Morishima, M. and Belsheim, J.A. (1999). Complaint Handling on the Shop Floor: Co-operative Relationships and Open-Minded Strategies. *The International Journal of Conflict Management* 10:45–68.

Voorhis, J. (1961). *American Co-operatives*. New York: Harper & Brothers Publishers.

Weber, M. (1946). *From Max Weber: Essays in Sociology*. Translated by H. Gerth and C.W. Mills. New York: Oxford University Press.

Wright, E.O. (2010). *Envisioning Real Utopias*. New York: Verso.

Zucker, L.G. (1977). The Role of Institutionalization in Cultural Persistence. *American Sociological Review* 42:726–743.

2

What is Workplace Dispute Resolution?

Workplaces are often sites of conflict, and workers' abilities to address these differences substantially affect the quality of their work experiences. This book explores whether co-op members are better able to address workplace disputes than their counterparts in conventional, hierarchical businesses.

Some research suggests that, by equalizing power, many difficulties of workplace dispute resolution—such as accessibility and mobilization—might be successfully resolved. Other literature rejects this possibility, implying that redistribution of power is not sufficient to circumvent fundamental problems of dispute resolution. Worker co-operatives provide living examples of these theories. As collectively owned entities with flattened hierarchies, co-operatives minimize official power inequities. Through egalitarian ideologies these workplaces attempt to equalize unofficial power. By focusing on mutual trust, co-operation, and worker empowerment, they endeavor to create a different environment for resolving disputes.

Legal Consciousness

Legal consciousness is the starting point for understanding dispute resolution. Scholars have defined legal consciousness as "the ways in which people make sense of law and legal institutions, that is, the understandings which give meaning to people's experiences and actions" (Ewick and Silbey 1992: 734.) Employees' daily activities incorporate their understandings of the world, their workplace and the rules and procedures that govern them as workers, creating legal consciousness.

Ewick and Silbey (1992: 46) explain that "(l)egal consciousness is produced and revealed in what people do as well as what they say." This study of legal consciousness examines what people report having done in the past and what they predict about their future behavior. In looking at their past and future behavior, interview subjects construct the boundaries of their legal consciousness (Ewick and Silbey 1998).

In constructing legal consciousness, people create meaning for themselves: what they name as actual harm, what they feel is appropriate blame, and which possible remedies they consider (Felstiner, Abel and Sarat 1980–81). But this is not done in isolation. Legal consciousness is collectively constructed and is constrained by its setting as well as by people's interpretations of meaning. As such, legal consciousness is an ever-changing, context-based concept, constantly altered by different experiences and interactions (Ewick and Silbey 1992).

Instead of focusing on laws and official legal actors, legal consciousness research examines "the meanings, sources of authority, and cultural practices that are commonly recognized as legal, regardless of who employs them or for what ends. In this rendering, people may invoke and enact legality in ways neither approved nor acknowledged by the law" (Ewick and Silbey 1998: 22). The legal consciousness framework recognizes that people interpret their experiences by drawing on a combination of law and other social structures (Sarat and Kearns 1995). These interpretations may be highly individualized, based on each person's social characteristics and their own previous contact with the law. Thus, some people might use the law to address social problems, while others in similar circumstances will hesitate to engage the law, even in harmful situations where the law purports to provide relief (Nielsen 2000). In this way, legal consciousness is each individual's "participation in this process of constructing legality" (Ewick and Silbey 1998: 45).

While this book examines internal company rules and formal grievance procedures rather than laws and courts, interviewees' legal consciousness within their workplace cultures is comparable to legal consciousness in the more traditional sense. For example, the rules and grievance procedures of the workplaces explored here are all associated with fairness, rule determinacy and rights—key symbols of law and legal authority (Sarat and Kearns 1995).

One way to explore legal consciousness is to examine the decision of whether or not to bring a lawsuit, or to file a formal grievance. Raising a formal grievance is not a simple decision. According to terminology developed by Felstiner, Abel, and Sarat, a worker must pass through several stages in order to raise a formal grievance. The first step is transforming the problem into a grievable dispute. To do this, the wronged party must realize that there is a problem ("naming" the perceived injurious experience). Then they must attribute the problem to another person, making the injurious experience into a grievance ("blaming"). Finally, they must bring the issue to the attention of the blamed party, seeking some remedy ("claiming"). A claim becomes a dispute when the blamed party rejects it in any way. To reach the formal stage, the dispute must be defined as public, and, therefore, as appropriate to be addressed in a non-private forum, specifically in the formal arena in question (Felstiner, Abel, and Sarat 1980–81).

However, the same power imbalances that allow wrongs to be committed also often prevent the victims from mobilizing against these actions (Bumiller 1988). Individual nature and social position combine to affect a victim's ability to transform an injurious experience into a dispute. Members of disempowered groups may have difficulty accomplishing the naming, blaming, and claiming stages because of the effects of the disparity of power and status that allowed the wrong to be perpetrated originally (Felstiner, Abel, and Sarat 1980–81). When naming, blaming, or claiming are considered inappropriate behavior or deemed "off-limits," (as they often are for less powerful groups), people cannot fully develop disputes or assert their rights; women often face this situation (Grillo 1991).

Conley and O'Barr (1990) studied people who lacked the ability to name problems which prevented them from bringing formal lawsuits, leaving them unable to address their problems in court. These people faced the hurdle of moving from "that was wrong" to "that was illegal" in their analyses of their issues. Yet, this linguistic leap must be made in order to claim a legal right. When this leap from naming something as "wrong" to naming it "illegal" was unmanageable, the would-be petitioners were unable to benefit from the court system (Conley and O'Barr 1990).

The blaming stage is also very important, because it identifies the party at whom the disputants can direct their actions. People who do not blame someone else for injurious experiences are less likely to voice displeasure about the injury. They are more likely to both define an experience as injurious and raise grievances if they can place blame upon another person (Felstiner,

Abel and Sarat 1980–81). Yet, Bumiller (1988) found that many people justify perpetrators' actions rather than placing blame on them.

Even if the victims accomplish both the naming and blaming, they might not be able to claim and seek remedies. For example, many victims may consider the primary measurement of success to be mere survival, not vindicating wrongful actions. These people may have successfully accomplished both the naming and blaming stages, but choose to avoid the claiming stage. This may be especially true if victims fear that taking action may actually worsen their predicament. Individuals might prefer the dignity of remaining anonymous over claiming their rights. In this regard, they avoid taking on the status of the victim, which may run counter to other self-concepts they may hold, such as being strong, independent, and able to "weather the storm" (Bumiller 1988).

Merry's work on legal consciousness found that "the ability to name and interpret is ... a central feature of the power exercised by those who handle problems" (Merry 1990: 4). In her study of courts and court mediators, she found that mediators and lower courts tried to reframe disputants' problems away from legal constructions and toward moral and therapeutic understandings. This strategy diverted disputants from using the courts and denied them the opportunity to have their injuries publicly declared "wrong." The disputants themselves resisted these attempts and tried to establish their own names for their problems (Merry 1990).

In analyzing the court mediators' efforts at reframing, Merry (1990) distinguishes three types of discourses: moralistic, legalistic, and therapeutic. Moralistic discourses focus on relationships, obligations, and responsibilities. Legalistic reframing places the dispute into "a discourse of property, of rights, of the protection of one's self and one's goods, of entitlement, of facts and truth" (Merry 1990: 6). Therapeutic discourses withhold judgment, but portray the offender as "lacking full responsibility for himself"; hence, compassionate, yet disempowering (Merry 1990: 8).

All three discourses are very potent ways of exerting control, although each is very different. By naming and reframing the disputes, the court mediators constrained the type of resolution available to the disputants. Merry asserts that "[t]he successful naming of an action or event within a particular discourse, thereby interpreting its meaning ... is an act of power" (1990: 4). Naming has powerful effects on disputants' legal consciousness, since it establishes which understandings will be privileged and what actions are considered appropriate (Merry 1990).

Workers' legal consciousness may be impeded or heightened by the structure and culture of their workplaces. Because of the emphasis on worker participation and empowerment in co-operatives, these organizations may have grievance cultures that encourage formal grievance resolution more so than conventional businesses. Nevertheless, heightened legal consciousness alone is not always sufficient to overcome various barriers to successful dispute resolution.

The workers at each company described in this book created grievance cultures that guided their naming of problems—naming, in particular, which responses were considered appropriate for each situation: formal grievances, informal resolution, self-help, or resignation. An important component of joining a company is learning the company's naming: understanding what is an appropriate formal grievance. While all companies in this study imparted their naming culture to their members, only some companies—such as Co-op Cab—had explicit ways of teaching new members the company's culture: as a result, the employees' understandings strongly affected their anticipated future behavior.

By examining legal consciousness in the workplace rather than in dispute-processing institutions such as courts or neighborhood mediators' offices, this book investigates perceptions of harm, blame, and appropriate remedy without the biases possibly imposed by drawing from subjects already present in dispute-processing settings. Because much of the legal consciousness research is conducted within dispute-processing institutions (Merry 1990; Sarat 1990), many interview subjects have already had their legal consciousness prompted and focused by their contact with these institutions before they become part of legal consciousness research (Marshall 2003). Therefore, their legal consciousness may be less characteristic than that of the general population.

The research in this book circumvented these methodological difficulties. People were interviewed in their workplaces and asked about a wide range of workplace issues. The interview topics included the culture of the company, jobs held, interpersonal dynamics, positive and negative aspects of the jobs, gender dynamics at work, and comparisons to previous jobs. The workplace, a familiar place for the interview subjects, is not associated specifically with dispute resolution or other legalistic procedures. Thus, in the same spirit as the work of Ewick and Silbey (1998), this study locates interview subjects who have not self-selected into the category of "grievants" and permits the interview subjects to share their "everyday" legal consciousness without focusing them on specific forums or events. The purpose of conducting these wide, loosely structured interviews was to avoid prompting subjects or suggesting responses about legal consciousness.

Barriers to Mobilization

Some scholars assert that structural rules, more so than individual qualities, promote activism (Pateman 1970). Pateman argues that workers in oligarchic organizations will be apathetic and passive, while workers in organizations that foster participation will respond with greater activism. Pateman maintains that people have a natural desire to control their own destinies, and, therefore, naturally prefer activism to passivity. People lack activism in oligarchic settings when they have not learned the necessary skills from prior participation in democratic organizations. She argues that, despite workers' natural tendency toward mobilization, without gaining the necessary skills for democratic participation, they will not demand participation (Pateman 1970).

Individuals who bring grievances in their workplace institutions often face the significant disadvantage of being "one-shot players," with few or no other experiences with the formal grievance procedures. The opponent, the management, is likely to be a "repeat player," one who has past and possibly ongoing experience in the arena (Galanter 1974). Galanter observed that in these situations, managers know what to expect and how to plan and strategize to maximize any possible advantages, using each case to influence the rules—both the general rules and content-specific ones. According to Galanter, the stakes are lower for repeat players than for each individual grievant. Management can afford to lose a few strategic cases, in order to claim the more important victories.

For the one-shotter, the case at hand is their only chance to win; they cannot cut their losses over the next several cases because there may be no other cases for them (Galanter 1974). However, this absence of concern about long-term effects gives the grievant a key advantage: they can "do their damnedest" without fear of reprisal the next time they go to court against the other party, because there will be no next time (Galanter 1974).

Bumiller explains that many people in her study did not pursue their claims because they "legitimized their own defeat" (Bumiller 1988: 29). Many did this by characterizing the struggle against perpetrators as "unwinnable" and "me against the corporation" (Ibid 1988: 52). In her work on the failure of anti-discrimination law to address racial and sexual oppression, Bumiller found that victims often felt defensive when they did confront their perpetrators, and felt as if the confrontation was a "double punishment" (Bumiller 1988: 52). They said that when they debated whether or not to initiate legal action, they "worried about their own guilt, as if they were charged with criminal offensives" (Bumiller 1988: 52). Victims said they preferred relating to their perpetrators as people, however ineffective this may be, to seeking help from the cold, bureaucratic law-enforcing authorities. They felt that raising discrimination claims would do more harm than any good they could accomplish (Bumiller 1988).

Moreover, the belief that authority is benevolent contributes to the more passive and accepting attitude of victims toward mistreatment by superiors, inhibiting naming and blaming. In this form of paternalism, victims fall back into an acceptance of conditions that inhibit their ability to move into the three grievance stages (Bumiller 1988).

Many of Bumiller's subjects found that the law itself reinforces their victimization and strengthens the very power divisions that enabled the initial mistreatment. Since many people who experience discrimination view the law as both protective and destructive, they fear that by publicly raising claims of mistreatment, they will lose whatever control they have over the situation, rather than gaining more power. The victims often justified their inaction by exaggerating the tyrannical power of their opponents, often managers and supervisors (Bumiller 1988).

Dispute resolution in worker co-operatives might be free of many of these obstacles. For example, because co-operatives emphasize equality and attempt to empower workers, victims might not see their causes as "unwinnable," as Bumiller's subjects did. However, members of co-operatives might be even more susceptible to abandoning their grievances due to a belief in a paternalistic benevolence on the part of the co-operative or fellow workers. Additionally, the co-operative itself might retain repeat-player status, while individual members with grievances could be considered one-shotters.

Procedural Justice

The level of procedural justice (how fair the process is by which one raises grievances or concerns) in organizations further complicates the issue of dispute resolution. Tyler and Lind (2000) assert that if disputants receive procedural justice, they are more willing to accept a wider range of distributive justice outcomes. Perceptions of procedural justice depend on whether the disputant trusts the authorities handling the dispute (trust), whether the disputant feels that they are seen by the authorities as a having full status in the group or society (standing), and whether the disputant believes that they received non-discriminatory, neutral treatment (neutrality) (Tyler and Lind 2000). If people feel that authorities are fair in their decision-making, then they believe they can obey orders without fear of exploitation. However, if authorities seem to act unfairly, obedience is less likely because people will fear abuse (Tyler and Lind 2000).

Tyler and Lind argue that people are more concerned about being rejected by authorities than they are about the outcome (distributive justice) of a specific dispute: "To lose any specific hoped-for outcome is a normal part of social life, but rejection by authorities carries the implication that one is less of a person than others." (Tyler and Lind 2000: 78). When people feel they have been treated fairly (procedural justice), they enter "group mode," which leads to co-operative behavior based on fairness. However, when people feel they have been treated poorly, they enter "individual mode," where they pattern their behavior to maximize short-term outcomes, rather than focusing on fairness. In addition, people who feel they have been treated very badly can develop a "vendetta response," ignoring any costs and focusing only on harming the instigator of the unfair treatment (Tyler and Lind 2000).

When people identify as members of the group the authorities represent they will be more willing to accept policies that are not in their immediate interest. However, Tyler and Lind add, "[t]hey're less influenced by procedural justice judgments when they identify more strongly with subgroups than with society and/or view the authorities as representatives of a group to which they do not belong" (Tyler and Lind 2000: 983).

Tyler and Lind assert that "the formal structures of the legal system make it more difficult for judges to communicate qualities of trustworthiness to disputants" (Tyler and Lind 2000: 85). People infer trustworthy motives when authorities act with informal discretion, more so than when those authorities enact formal rules. Informal justice allows authorities to communicate their trustworthiness more so because informal dispute resolution allows them to engage in more discretionary actions. Thus, in informal settings outside the court, authorities have more freedom and flexibility to communicate their "benevolent motives and caring attitudes" toward disputants, and hence are seen as more trustworthy (Tyler and Lind 2000: 85).

Exit, Voice, and Loyalty

In his influential 1970s book, *Exit, Voice, and Loyalty*, Albert O. Hirschman asserted that three options exist for employees who are dissatisfied with their job: they can leave the firm (exit); they can express their dissatisfaction to the relevant authority (voice); or they can stay in the situation without taking action (acquiescence). This study operationalizes "acquiescence" as the category "toleration," meaning that the problem is perceived but no action is taken. Only voice and exit provide the feedback that enables organizations to improve. When the exit option is unavailable, the only way dissatisfied people can communicate their frustration is by using voice, so that "the role of voice would increase as the opportunities for exit decline," according to Hirschman (1970: 34). In situations where one cannot exit or the cost of exit is particularly high (such as membership in one's family, state, or church), the voice option is the only way to express displeasure.

When both quitting and speaking up are viable options, the decision to exit or remain will be affected by how effective workers believe their voices are. Hirschman writes that if workers "are sufficiently convinced that voice will be effective, then they may well postpone exit ... [T]herefore, exit can also be viewed as depending on the ability and willingness of the [workers] to take up the voice option ... [since] once you have exited, you have lost the opportunity for voice, but not vice versa" (Hirschman 1970: 37). Other research, such as that on whistle-blowers, demonstrates that sometimes workers go outside their organization and speak up only after their voices have been ignored by their supervisors (Rothschild and Miethe 1999).

Hirschman argues that exit is closely linked to voice, and that the concept of loyalty is key to understanding which conditions favor exit versus voice. Sometimes loyalty is defined as a possible action, similar to acquiescence, while others read Hirschman as defining loyalty as a contingency that shapes outcomes, rather than an outcome itself (Dowding et al. 2000: 447). This book defines loyalty as allegiance to a concept outside of the self, such as an organization. The presence or absence of loyalty affects what courses of action individuals will choose, such as whether to continue in an unpleasant circumstance and voice their unhappiness or to exit the objectionable environment.

When Hirschman defines "loyalty" as loyalty to the organization, he posits that people who have an exit option will stay and, instead, engage in voice if they're willing to forgo the certainty of exit and embrace the uncertainty of possible improvement and if they believe they can influence the organization. In this way, "loyalty holds exit at bay and activates voice," in that it lessens the attractive ease of exiting by raising the cost of exit, making the exertion needed for voice less unappealing (Hirschman 1970: 78). Yet voice is most effective when "backed up by the threat of exit" (Hirschman 1970: 82).

High entry costs can affect the timing of voice and exit, although Hirschman emphasizes that high entry costs do not cause acquiescence, but, instead, promote greater voice. Those who have paid dearly to enter will be both disinclined to exit readily or to stay and remain passive, but rather will seek to address problems. High exit costs might have a similar effect.

Hirschman's loyalty is often only applied within the context of the organization, that is, loyalty to the firm itself. Other times, however, researchers examine loyalty that extends beyond an organization to an industry or to industry-related ideals or goals. For example, Perrucci et al. (1980) examined whistle-blowing and found that sometimes employees may have less loyalty to a specific firm, but more loyalty to the industry or to certain ideals.

Other researchers have explored concepts similar to loyalty, such as allegiance, commitment, and attachment. This study's specific definition of loyalty is somewhat similar to Meyer and Allen's definition of organizational commitment, which describes commitment as having three components: affective, normative, and continuance. They define affective commitment as an employee's emotional attachment to, and identification with, the workplace. Normative commitment refers to commitment out of obligation or feelings of moral responsibility. Continuance commitment—the more rational-choice, cost-benefit component of commitment—is defined as commitment to the organization because the employee needs the income of that job (Meyer and Allen 1997).

The definition of organizational loyalty this book uses somewhat parallels this definition of commitment. Loyalty, as an allegiance to a concept outside the self (as mentioned previously), has two components: an emotional/affective component and a goal-allegiance component. The emotional/affective component mirrors the affective component outlined by Meyer and Allen: it involves workers' identification with—and emotional attachment to—their workplaces. The goal-allegiance component addresses the loyalty employees feel toward an organization when that entity exemplifies or aligns with their own broader goals. An example of this type of loyalty would be the worker who feels strongly about the environment and recycling waste and feels great commitment to his recycling job because it's in accordance with his goals regarding improving the environment. This book's theory of organizational loyalty does not have a component that parallels continuance commitment, since loyalty in this context is conceptualized as allegiance that surpasses more self-focused concerns, such as personal income.

Alternative Dispute Resolution

Some employees choose to resolve workplace disputes outside the courts. Any dispute process other than litigation (which takes place in the courts) can be classified as alternative dispute resolution (ADR). ADR can take several forms: extremely formal arbitration with the use of separate lawyers for each side and a neutral, judge-like arbitrator; informal mediation in which a separate, but knowledgeable, person assists the two disputing parties to find a mutually agreeable solution; or grievance procedures within a workplace where the mediator is a specialist employee of the workplace (internal dispute resolution). ADR has many advocates and many critics, both of whom use comparisons between ADR and the courts for their arguments.

Advocates of ADR argue that ADR is better than the courts at addressing the needs and interests of parties because it provides a more expansive array of remedies and redresses a broader spectrum of problems. Through ADR, parties can explore their true interests and the sources of their problems, in addition to agreeing to a resolution to the issue at hand (Menkle-Meadow 1984). ADR can provide solutions to parties who may have no legal right, but who do have a legitimate claim. In this way, ADR can fashion more creative solutions than courts are at liberty to offer. ADR is also said to be more efficient and less expensive for participants. Advocates also argue that the ADR process is less adversarial and produces greater satisfaction (Bush 1989).

The most powerful criticism of ADR is its tendency to diminish the importance of the rights of each party (Silbey and Sarat 1989). Many argue that rights are vital for people who enjoy little social or political power and should not be compromised for procedural convenience (Crenshaw 1988). Villmore and others argue that rights powerfully legitimize the experiences of disempowered groups in society. In addition to directly ignoring legal rights, ADR processes can undermine rights by altering how the issues of grievances are framed, circumventing rights indirectly (Edelman, Erlanger, and Lande 1993; Silbey and Sarat 1989).

Furthermore, the emphasis on compromise, present in many forms of ADR, undermines both rights and the broader policies behind those rights (Silbey and Sarat 1989). The definition of compromise is that each side gives up some portion of that to which it feels entitled. However, if one party is basing its understanding of its entitlement on legal rights, and the other on some other rationalization, then a compromise between these two positions inherently erodes the legal rights at issue.

Another important criticism of ADR is that it is easily influenced by power differentials based on class, race and gender (Delgado et al. 1985; Grillo 1991). Classism, racism, and sexism are prevalent throughout society, and often ADR lacks the formal protections that the courts provide, thereby reinforcing certain parties' privileged and powerful positions. The formality of adjudication—along with the advocacy and distancing provided by legal representation—might not only provide better protection against abuse of party inequalities (Delgado et al. 1985), but may also distance parties from the site of confrontation sufficiently to create a buffer that makes the dispute resolution less taxing and emotional (Grillo 1991).

Internal Dispute Resolution

Disputes resolved within organizations involve many of the same advantages and disadvantages as ADR. Because internal dispute resolution is situated within the workplace, it is more accessible and somewhat more familiar to employees. Because it is handled by the employer, it is often less expensive and more efficient, as well as being open to "extra-legal" options (Edelman, Erlanger, and Lande 1993).

One chief concern with internal dispute resolution, however, is that it may make employees less likely to use adjudication to address their disputes. If employees believe that the employer's grievance resolution system is effective and easily accessible—while the courts are perceived as frightening, expensive, and unknown—they may be more inclined to utilize the internal dispute resolution process, ignoring their right to bring lawsuits. This means that these employees will not be able to resolve issues with the benefit of a trained advocate or an objective third party. Private resolution also has larger consequences not only for the disputants, but also for other employees. Privately resolved disputes receive little publicity; therefore they do not raise the consciousness of others in similar situations. Thus, grievances resolved internally lack the larger benefit of facilitating future naming and blaming (Felstiner, Abel, and Sarat 1980–81). Internal dispute resolution also has little, if any, precedent-setting power, forcing each disputant to argue their position anew, even where others have previously pursued the same line successfully (Edelman, Erlanger, and Lande 1993).

In addition to the perpetuation of societal inequalities, internal dispute resolution also exacerbates inequalities created within the organization by imposing the workplace's hierarchy of power on the dispute resolution procedure (Edelman, Erlanger, and Lande 1993). Within the workplace, the employer enjoys a structural position of privilege and power, as well as the advantage of being a repeat player, as discussed above (Galanter 1974). Given such unequal positions, employees are often hesitant to raise disputes against their employers (Bumiller 1988; Felstiner, Abel, and Sarat 1980–81; Miller and Sarat 1981).

Moreover, internal dispute resolution further heightens employers' advantages by inhibiting employees from challenging their employers. Because of its official nature (which sometimes mimics courtroom proceedings), internal dispute resolution symbolizes justice and legality, thereby providing legitimacy to the employers and their practices. Within the organization, this legitimization makes it more difficult for employees to raise issues because the internal dispute processes serve to reaffirm the employers' position as unquestionably correct. Externally, an employee may find it more difficult to convince agencies or officials that their employer has wronged them (Edelman, Erlanger, and Lande 1993).

The courts, also, are affected by organizations' internal dispute resolution procedures. As internal dispute resolution procedures become increasingly prevalent, courts accept these procedures as adequate substitutes for the legal process (Edelman, Uggen, and Erlanger 1999). This transfer of power occurs without the courts seriously questioning the fairness of these procedures, which lack any legal content or rights focus (Edelman, Erlanger, and Lande 1993).

Co-operative Interdependence

Some researchers, including Brett and Goldberg, emphasize that interest-based, rather than rights-focused bargaining significantly increases successful grievance handling. Interest-based bargaining occurs when both sides perceive themselves "on the same side," working toward the same goals. This perception is sometimes referred to as co-operative interdependence.

Tjosvold, Morishima, and Belsheim identified three types of goal interdependencies: co-operation, when people believe their goals are positively linked; competition, when people believe that goal attainment by others diminishes the likelihood of their own goal attainment; and independence, when people believe that their goals are unrelated. Workers in co-operation expect each person to work hard toward the shared goals; therefore, these workers are more likely to exchange information and support each other and to form strong interpersonal relationships. Workers in competition are more likely to restrict information, distort communication, and promote their own interests to the detriment of others' interests. Independent workers act similarly to the workers in competition, but with weaker effects and with greater indifference toward fellow workers (Tjosvold, Morishima, and Belsheim 1999).

Tjosvold, Morishima, and Belsheim argue that co-operative goals—in contrast to competitive and independent goals—promote open-minded discussions of disputes that result in resolutions that mutually benefit both supervisors and employees. Developing co-operative goals and open-minded negotiation skills can help supervisors and employees to create integrative solutions to shop-floor conflicts (Tjosvold, Morishima, and Belsheim 1999). In addition, the researchers found that employees and supervisors that experienced co-operative interdependence "were able to negotiate open-mindedly to develop integrative solutions that successfully handled their informal grievances" while workers in competitive interdependence were "closed-mouthed, inefficient, dismissed new ideas, and developed solutions that worked against employee interests" (Tjosvold, Morishima, and Belsheim

1999: 59). Co-operative interdependence led to shared understandings of issues, common objectives, and trust that both sides want a solution for mutual benefit. Supervisors and employees were often willing to compromise, assist each other, and work for a successful resolution to problems: "By emphasizing their cooperative goals and discussing issues flexibly, supervisors and employees reached solutions that benefited them both" (Tjosvold, Morishima, and Belsheim 1999: 60).

Tjosvold, Morishima, and Belsheim's study of co-operative interdependence echoes aspects of Tyler and Lind's analysis of procedural justice. Workers in businesses employing co-operative interdependence experience greater trust and acceptance from their supervisors. Assuming that these workers also experience greater neutrality, as disputants they would enjoy high levels of procedural justice. Thus, it might follow that workers and managers with co-operative interdependence would resolve disputes more easily than others.

Dispute Resolution in Worker Co-operatives

When the structure of the organization is flattened, as it is in worker co-operatives, dispute resolution strategies might be different. Indeed, Wright asserts that co-operatives may be "potentially more efficient and productive than capitalist firms" in part because of "the collaborative processes within a cooperative can enhance its problem-solving capacities" (Wright 2010: 168). Some scholars reason that worker co-operatives exemplify the type of workplaces where co-operative interdependence (Tjosvold, Morishima, and Belsheim 1999: 60)—along with organizationally encouraged activism (Pateman 1970)—would most likely be found. For example, workers and managers in co-operatives may be more likely to share similar goals than employees and managers in more conventional, hierarchical settings.

Researchers are only beginning to study grievances and dispute resolution in these non-conventional businesses. Several books on alternative businesses briefly address dispute resolution. Denning's work, *The Practice of Workplace Participation* (1998), mentions barriers to resolving disputes in flattened organizations. The three companies he studied ranged in their elements of worker involvement and ownership: one had a powerful management structure but workers were partially compensated in stock; another was smaller, yet it mainly encouraged worker involvement by offering stock ownership; and a third was a large manufacturing plant whose *managers* primarily bought out the company rather than see it close. Not surprisingly, he found "the firm and the worker ... [were] caught between conflicting messages" and reported tension among workers over insufficient access to information about the company (Denning 1998: 150).

Worker Participation and Ownership, by Whyte et al. (1983), includes information about work stoppages and other types of extreme action in their research on labor-management committees in several private and public organizations in Jamestown, a small industrial city. However, their main focus is not on workplace conflict and dispute resolution, but on co-operative strategies for strengthening local economies. Greater analysis of workplace conflicts and disputes appears in *Job-Saving Strategies: Worker Buyouts and QWL*, by Hochner et al. (1988), who explain that worker participation can both decrease and transform disputes; while certain disputes are fewer, others are more frequent, such as disputes over long-term planning and use of resources. Lindenfeld and Rothschild-Whitt include a chapter by Mansbridge on conflict in their book, *Workplace Democracy and Change* (Mansbridge 1982), which primarily focuses on members' fear of conflict, rather than on dispute resolution. Mansbridge's study of a 41-person counseling co-operative found that members often tried to avoid conflict, rather than addressing problems directly. Members avoided open conflict in the public meeting by gathering earlier and agreeing to act and vote in similar ways. Although this strategy allowed for much public unanimity, it also alienated newcomers and others not connected to the informal power networks.

Stuart Henry's work in the early 1980s specifically examined dispute resolution in worker co-operatives. His research examined dispute resolution in various types of organizations, including two types of co-operatives: housing co-operatives and worker co-operatives (Henry 1983). His work explored the range of ways people in different settings use public law and private dispute resolution (referred to as "Private Justice," also the title of the book). Henry found that co-operatives had "executive-elite decision-making of the kind found in hierarchically organized companies" and relied on state law, in contrast to their ideology, to avoid state intervention. He reports that co-operatives are viable alternatives to conventional institutions but that they operationalize justice imperfectly, often in contrast with their co-operative ideals (Henry 1983).

Although this research produced rich data, the results from the two types of co-operatives are not separated: Members of housing co-operatives and producer/worker co-operatives are quoted interchangeably. In some ways, this method produces a lively, intricate story. However, it also results in an unclear picture of the circumstances of these two types of co-operatives. Conceivably, housing and producer/worker co-operatives have significant differences that affect their dispute resolution behaviors: (1) the purpose of the co-operative, which could affect members' goals, purposes for joining, and attitudes toward dispute resolution options; (2) the manner and the amount of time members share each other's company, which affects how they interact, and, potentially how they resolve disputes; and (3) the ease of informal member confrontation and exiting, which would contribute to the range of dispute-resolutions options available. Without separating this data, Henry does not confirm (or dispel) the saliency of these differences, nor does he allow the audience to understand the differences between these two types of co-operative organizations. Nevertheless, Henry's work opens the door for investigation into power, justice, and grievances in organizations that attempt to equalize power.

Two more recent books take the torch from Henry and explore dispute resolution in flattened, employee-owned businesses. Kleinman's work, *Opposing Ambitions* (1996), includes an analysis of how members of Renewal, an alternative health center, address disputes. Tucker's recent book, *The Therapeutic Corporation* (1999), examines conflict resolution in a large employee-owned manufacturing corporation. Kleinman uses theories of gender and power to analyze her data; Tucker applies Donald Black's paradigm of "pure sociology" to grievance behavior at his research site. Although neither book defines their sites as worker co-operatives, the authors studied businesses with shared ownership and shared management by the workers. Kleinman's site embraces the concept of shared management more strongly than it does shared ownership, with members intricately and thoroughly involved in the management of the health center; Kleinman does not discuss ownership, probably because ownership is not a key issue for members of Renewal. As a not-for-profit that rents its space, Renewal owns little capital and is often in debt. (Nevertheless, from the unequal distribution of wages, one can surmise that if there were profits to share, the distribution would not be equitable.) Conversely, Tucker's research site embraces shared ownership more strongly than it does shared managerial decision-making, with more limited employee involvement in managerial decisions. Also, while both are innovative organizations that try to create more egalitarian workplaces, neither business is devoid of power inequalities.

In her study of Renewal, Kleinman focuses on power and the issue of equality in a flat, non-hierarchical organization. Most, but not all, of the practitioners were men, and all of the staff members were women. Practitioners received about $30 an hour for their services, a portion of which they kept for themselves; the rest was turned over to Renewal. Staff workers were paid $4 dollars an hour, but often were not paid at all; Renewal did not make enough money to pay the staff members. Thus, Renewal clearly had a two-class division within its membership—a division that split roughly along gender lines. Much of Kleinman's analysis focuses on the differences in power and status that resulted from this situation. Since there were fewer than two dozen workers at Renewal, members resolved disputes informally, through direct confrontation, at board and member meetings, and at retreats. (In fact, Kleinman does not mention any formal internal procedure.)

The members' professed ideology of progressive and egalitarian ideals, ironically, made dispute resolution more difficult for the female staff members. Although the members described themselves as progressive and were conscious of some forms of societal power, they did little to lessen the inequalities between practitioners and non-practitioners and between men and women. Because the members of the organization saw their very presence in an alternative business as "proof" of the practitioners' enlightenment, the staff and female volunteers had difficulty directly raising their complaints around issues of inequality. Additionally, the members saw Renewal as a community rather than as a job and found any rights consciousness particularly difficult. Although the women did occasionally acknowledge these concerns, they didn't achieve effective change.

The difficulties in dispute resolution at Renewal can be clarified using Felstiner, Abel, and Sarat's (1980–81) stages of disputing (naming, blaming, claiming), although Kleinman does not refer to this work specifically. These women often were unable to name their issues as problems, viewing them as their personal concerns. They were unable to blame, misperceiving practitioners' commitment to alternative medicine as a commitment to shared power and equality. And they were powerless to claim, because their workplace culture made it difficult to acknowledge their criticisms as legitimate. In particular, the female staff workers viewed many of their concerns as their own fault for inappropriately taking issues personally. For example, feeling unappreciated when scarce income went to practitioners instead of to the staff was labeled as inappropriately focusing on money, rather than as a legitimate complaint about inequity in a supposedly egalitarian organization.

Tucker applies Donald Black's paradigm of "pure sociology," to examine an organization he calls HelpCo, where all employees owned stock and were allowed greater information about – and some input into – managerial decision-making. HelpCo is a "high-technology company that designs, manufactures, and repairs electronic components for the telecommunications industry" (Tucker 1999: 21). HelpCo employed almost two hundred workers; 61 of whom Tucker interviewed. The company culture was very informal: everyone, including the president, used their first names only; office dress, such as neckties, was not common. In describing HelpCo, Tucker emphasized its commitment to sharing power, by allowing employee teams to be responsible for making various decisions ("equality"); the many similarities among workers, such as race (white), class (middle) and interests (electronics) ("homogeneity"); and the strong interpersonal ties both within and outside departments ("intimacy"). Blackian theory, arguing that therapy will thrive when there is equality, homogeneity, and intimacy, predicts that therapy is likely to be used in an organization like HelpCo (Tucker 1999). Tucker identified all three of these components at HelpCo and confirmed Black's prediction that an organization with these three traits would rely on therapy to solve disputes, finding that HelpCo is, in fact, a "therapeutic corporation" (Tucker 1999).

By describing this organization as having a therapeutic orientation toward problems, Blackian theory means that individuals are given help and treatment, rather than punishment. Throughout, Tucker uses Black's conceptual framework of social space to explain why therapy is frequently used at HelpCo (Black 1995). Black's theory of therapy, the focus of Tucker's book, fits within Tucker's theory of third-party intervention, which asserts "the likelihood and degree of authoritative and partisan intervention by third parties varies directly [1] with the amount of inequality and social distance between adversaries and [2] with the superiority and social remoteness of third parties" (Black 1995: 834–837).

Conclusion

These past studies imply that organizing workplaces as worker co-operatives may make a substantial difference in workers' lives. However, these studies also demonstrate that successful dispute resolution is not guaranteed in co-operatives, despite many strategies designed to facilitate success. Structural and individualistic hurdles exist that deter potential disputants from initiating grievances and resolving their disputes satisfactorily. However, some factors, including greater trust and co-operative interdependence, might facilitate easier and more successful grievance resolution. One does expect these factors to be more common in worker co-operatives, where inclusion, equality, and worker participation are officially encouraged.

Works Cited

Black, D. (1995). The Epistemology of Pure Sociology. *Law & Social Inquiry* 20:829–870.

Bumiller, K. (1988). *The Civil Rights Society: The Social Construction of Victims*. Baltimore: The John Hopkins University Press.

Bush, R.A.B. (1989). Defining Quality in Dispute Resolution. *Denver University Law Review* 66:335–367.

Conley, J.M. and O'Barr, W.M. (1990). *Rules versus Relationships: The Ethnography of Legal Discourse*. Chicago: The University of Chicago Press.

Crenshaw, K. (1988). Race, Reform and Retrenchment: Transformation and Legitimation in Antidiscrimination Law. *Harvard Law Review* 101:1131–1387.

Delgado, R., Dunn, D., Brown, P., Lee, H. and Hubbert, D. (1985). Fairness and Formality: Minimizing the Risk of Prejudice in Alternative Dispute Resolution. *Wisconsin Law Review* 1985:585–629.

Denning, S.L. (1998). *The Practice of Workplace Participation*. Westport, Connecticut: Quorum Books.

Dowding, K., John, P., Mergoupis, T. and Van Vugt, M. (2000). Exit, Voice and Loyalty: Analytic and Empirical Developments. *European Journal of Political Research* 37:469–495.

Edelman, L.B., Erlanger, H.S. and Lande, J. (1993). Internal Dispute Resolution: The Transformation of Civil Rights in the Workplace. *Law and Society Review* 27:497–534.

Edelman, L.B., Uggen, C. and Erlanger, H.S. (1999). The Endogeneity of Legal Regulation: Grievance Procedures as Rational Myth. *American Journal of Sociology* 105:406–454.

Ewick, P. and Silbey, S.S. (1998). *The Common Place of Law*. Chicago: University of Chicago Press.

Ewick, P. and Silbey, S.S. (1992). Conformity, Contestation, and Resistance: An Account of Legal Consciousness. *New England Law Review* 26:731–749.

Felstiner, W.L.F., Abel, R.L. and Sarat, A. (1980–81). The Emergence and Transformation of Disputes: Naming, Blaming, Claiming… *Law and Society Review* 15:631–654.

Galanter, M. (1974). Why the 'Haves' Come Out Ahead: Speculations on the Limits of Legal Change. *Law & Society Review* 9:95–127.

Grillo, T. (1991). The Mediation Alternative: Process Dangers for Women. *Yale Law Journal* 100:1545–1610.

Henry, S. (1983). *Private Justice: Towards Integrated Theorising in the Sociology of Law*. London: Routledge & Kegan Paul.

Hirschman, A.O. (1970). *Exit, Voice, and Loyalty: Responses to Declines in Firms, Organizations, and States*. Cambridge: Harvard University Press.

Hochner, A., Granrose, C.S., Goode, J., Simon, E. and Appelbaum, E. (1988). *Worker Buyouts and QWL*: W. E. Upjohn Institute for Employment Research.

Kleinman, S. (1996). *Opposing Ambitions: Gender and Identity in an Alternative Organization*. Chicago: University of Chicago Press.

Mansbridge, J.J. (1982). Fears of Conflict in Face-to-Face Democracies. pp. 213–256 in *Workplace Democracy and Change*, edited by F. Lindenfeld and J. Rothschild-Whitt. Boston, MA: Extending Horizons Books.

Marshall, A.M. (2003). Injustice Frames, Legality, and the Everyday Construction of Sexual Harassment. *Law & Social Inquiry* 28:659–689.

Menkle-Meadow, C. (1984). Toward Another View of Legal Negotiations: The Structure of Problem Solving. *UCLA Law Review* 31:754–789.

Merry, S.E. (1990). The Discourses of Mediation and the Power of Naming. *Yale Journal of Law & the Humanities* 2:1–36.

Meyer, J.P. and Allen, N.J. (1997). *Commitment in the Workplace: Theory, Research, and Application*. Thousand Oaks, CA: Sage Publications.

Miller, R.E. and Sarat, A. (1981). Grievances, Claims, and Disputes: Assessing the Adversary Culture. *Law and Society Review* 15:525–561.

Nielsen, L.B. (2000). Situating Legal Consciousness: Experiences and Attitudes of Ordinary Citizens about Law and Street Harassment. *Law and Society Review* 34:1056–1090.

Pateman, C. (1970). *Participation and Democratic Theory*. London: Cambridge University Press.

Perrucci, R., Anderson, R.M., Schendel, D.E. and Trachtman, L.E. (1980). Whistle-Blowing: Professionals' Resistance to Organiational Authority. *Social Problems* 28:149–164.

Rothschild, J. and Miethe, T.M. (1999). Whistle-Blower Disclosures and Management Retaliation: The Battle to Control Information About Organization Corruption. *Work and Occupations* 26:107–128.

Sarat, A. (1990). '...The Law is All Over': Power, Resistance and the Legal Consciousness of the Welfare Poor. *Yale Journal of Law & the Humanities* 2:343–379.

Sarat, A. and Kearns, T.R. (1995). Beyond the Great Divide: Forms of Legal Scholarship and Everyday Life. in *Law in Everyday Life*, edited by A.S. a. T.R. Kearns. Ann Arbor: The University of Michigan Press.

Silbey, S. and Sarat, A. (1989). Dispute Processing in Law and Legal Scholarship: From Institutional Critique to the Reconstruction of the Judicial Subject. *Denver University Law Review* 66:437–487.

Tjosvold, D., Morishima, M. and Belsheim, J.A. (1999). Complaint Handling on the Shop Floor: Co-operative Relationships and Open-Minded Strategies. *The International Journal of Conflict Management* 10:45–68.

Tucker, J. (1999). *The Therapeutic Corporation*. New York: Oxford University Press.

Tyler, T.R. (2000). Multiculturalism and the Willingness of Citizens to Defer to Law and to Legal Authorities. *Law & Social Inquiry* 25.

Tyler, T.R. and Lind, E.A. (2000). Procedural Justice. pp. 65–92 in *Handbook of Justice Research in Law*, edited by J. Sanders and V.L. Hamilton. New York: Kluwer Academic/Plenum Publishers.

Wright, E.O. (2010). *Envisioning Real Utopias.* New York: Verso.

Whyte, W.F., Hammer, T.H., Meek, C.B., Nelson, R. and Stern, R.N. (1983). *Worker Participation and Ownership*. Ithaca, N.Y.: ILR Press.

3

Three Different Worker Co-operatives

The research featured in this book employed the comparative case method (Ragin 1987) to explore dispute resolution strategies and attitudes among workers in three industries: coal mining, taxicab driving, and organic food distribution. Within each industry, I conducted interviews and observed a worker co-operative and a matched conventional business. The industries in this study offered a range of workplace cultures, gender balances, and business objectives. I visited each business twice, achieving variation in interviewees on many dimensions. The duration of these visits ranged from several days to two weeks.

All businesses in this study met several key criteria: first, the company needed to have a formal system for grievance resolution. Second, it had to be large enough that a formal grievance system was necessary; the minimum size was 30 workers. Third, each business had to be a stable organization with established procedures; none was fewer than two years old. Fourth, no organization could be part of a larger organization. Additionally, each co-operative included in the study had to be a true worker co-operative—with all employees being equal shareholders and no outside shareholders—not merely an Employee Stock Option Plan (ESOP) company.

I conducted a total of 128 interviews: 18 at HealthBite Distributors, 35 at Organix Co-op, 14 at Private Taxi, 20 at Co-op Cab, and 41 at Coal Co-operative/ Valley Colliery. (Coal Co-operative and Valley Colliery were the same physical mine, but under different ownership and management systems, as explained below.) For each site, Table 3.1 provides summary statistics on the interviewees as well as on the organizations. I did not identify a specific group of workers whom I knew to have had "disputes" but spoke to all interviewees about their workplace experiences. I included a wide variety of interviewees to maximize the range of problems and experiences as well as the variety of solutions and expectations. My sample included present and former employees as well as managers and worker-managers. Interviewees also differed in terms of length of employment, sex, race, age, level of education, socioeconomic status, and job classification. Through careful sampling and the repetition of responses I encountered as interviewees spoke of similar themes, I have become confident that my findings are well triangulated and valid. Although these interviewees are not statistically representative of all the workers at their individual organizations, the diversity of this sample is helpful for developing conceptual models.

Table 3.1   Summary of sites and interviewees

	Industry	Type of organization	Location	Number of workers	Number interviewed
Valley Colliery	coal mine	conventional	Wales (U.K.)	252	38** (15%)
Coal Co-operative	coal mine	worker co-operative	Wales (U.K.)	239	41** (17%)
Private Taxi	taxicab driving	conventional	Wisconsin (U.S.)	120	14 (12%)
Co-op Cab	taxicab driving	worker co-operative	Wisconsin (U.S.)	150	20 (13%)
HealthBite Distributors	organic food	conventional	London (U.K.)	32	18 (56%)
Organix Co-op	organic food	worker co-operative	Halifax (U.K.)	50	35 (70%)

Note: ** There is substantial overlap with these two sets of workers, because Valley Colliery and Coal Co-operative were the same mine at different time periods.

Generally, I approached interviewees myself, rather than requesting volunteers to come forward. Sometimes I would approach a group of people, ask to talk with one of them, and schedule interview times with the others. Other times I would approach people who were off by themselves. Since a significant focus of this study is the raising of grievances, interviewing only those inclined to step forward could create an unrepresentative sample of perspectives on grievance behavior. The assertiveness and extroversion necessary to volunteer to be interviewed by a stranger may correlate with attitudes on raising grievances and the ability to resolve disputes. I arranged certain interviews in advance with key people and workers from under-represented groups within the organization whom I wanted to be certain to include. Most of the interviews were conducted in public places or in private spaces at the companies themselves. All interviews were conducted in person, using a set of open-ended questions as initial probes on a wide variety of work-related topics.

Coal Mining

The nature of coal mining makes miners a cohesive group. Workers rely on one another, not only for production but also for safety. And miners share a history of labor struggles and hardship (Dennis, Henriques, and Slaughter 1956). Often physically removed from larger towns and cities and emotionally isolated by anti-miner prejudice, miners and their families historically have kept to themselves and are quite loyal to one another: "Miners were often seen as a race apart from other workers. Hardship created a community spirit hardly equaled in other industries," writes one historian (Pump-House-Museum 1997). As one fourth-generation miner in this study said:

> It's a very close-knit community. I live 25 miles from here, and I know if any of the boys come down to my neck of the woods for a night out and a crowd of boys start punching on me, they'll be in there. Doesn't matter whether they are outnumbered or not. If a factory worker goes out, and is set upon, the factory boys may help out in a fight situation. But if you find a couple of boys picking on any miner, you will find a crowd of miners.

This contrast between mining culture and that of other industries was also felt on the job, as this electrician explained:

> People here are prepared to pitch in. No one will walk past you if you're struggling. There's always someone [who] will offer to give you a hand. Outside, you'll probably find that if something's your job in a trade industry, it's your job, and you [alone] get on with it.

Many miners spoke with disdain about factory work, recalling when they had to take jobs in factories between the time of Valley mine closing and its reopening as a worker co-operative. Not only did they find the culture atomistic with little solidarity compared to that of the mining industry, but they also felt they had much less freedom and autonomy than they did in coal mining. Several miners said they hated having to stand in one place in factories or having to raise their hands to get permission to go to the bathroom. Even though miners worked in groups, they maintained a certain level of personal autonomy.

The British mining industry has been known for its labor-management struggles, most notably the serious strikes of 1911, 1921, 1926, 1972, and 1974 (Dennis, Henriques, and Slaughter 1956). Perhaps the worst strike was the 1984–5 strike, a bitterly fought struggle against an anticipated colliery closure program (Sunderland Museum 1997). The much-feared closures did happen, despite an otherwise healthy coal industry and deep reserves of coal. The experience [of the closures] transformed the attitudes and expectations of the whole nation. In 1996, fewer than 30 [coal-mining] pits were still working in Britain and substantial reserves of coal have been permanently abandoned (Sunderland Museum 1997). These closures devastated villages for which coal mining was the primary, if not the only, industry. As one museum exhibit on mining said, 'Mining families knew that their community was brought into existence only to obtain the coal from beneath their feet. Their future would have as much continuity as the flow of coal' (Sunderland Museum 1997).

Mines were privately owned in the United Kingdom until 1947, when the National Coal Board was set up to take the place of the previous mine owners. One of the intended effects of nationalization of the coal industry was to allow greater worker involvement in the way the mines were run; the board set up guidelines for joint consultation and formed a committee, comprised of equal numbers of management representatives and miners' representatives (Dennis, Henriques, and Slaughter 1956). This worker-management collaboration, however, did not succeed. Instead, "[the miners] saw no change in the local management of the mines when nationalization took place. In all these ways, they [saw] themselves opposed to the same forces as before nationalization" (Dennis, Henriques, and Slaughter 1956: 77).

VALLEY COLLIERY AND COAL CO-OPERATIVE

Valley Colliery and Coal Co-operative are deep-pit mines, producing high-grade, highly marketable anthracite coal (Watson 1996). Deep-pit mining— in contrast to strip mining—involves going deep underground to remove coal. This type of mining is much more dangerous and, in some ways, more expensive than strip mining, where the top layers of ground are removed and only the coal near the surface is extracted. Deep-pit mining is the type of mining that many people envision when they think of mining: elevator cages taking miners down a deep shaft to work, helmets with lamps attached to provide light underground, and lunch tins sufficiently airtight to keep out coal dust and vermin. The images of underground explosions, lucky miners covered with black coal dust, and less-lucky miners with missing body parts, belong to this type of mining. While the level of safety in the mines has improved over the years, it continues to be a concern. In fact, the members of Coal Co-operative spoke of safety as their highest priority.

The miners took many safety precautions. Each miner carried an emergency kit in the event of a gas leak or explosion, wore safety shoes, and had access to dust-filtering masks and protective goggles. The levels of poisonous gasses were closely monitored and kept well below the industry minimum standard, and fresh air was constantly circulated through the use of giant fans and ventilation doors. Metal discs identifying each miner were kept at the mine's entrance and were collected when he exited to ensure that no one was ever left inside. Although all gasses were monitored electronically, a cage of canaries was still kept in the lamp room, as a reminder of the earlier relationship between these birds and miners' safety.

The type of deep-pit mining practiced at Valley Colliery and Coal Co-operative is called retreat mining, and is considered the safer type of deep-pit mining. In retreat mining, two corridors are drilled down to the end of a seam. The corridors are then joined; here is where the mining of that seam begins. Rather than digging deeper and deeper into the mine to excavate that seam's coal, retreat mining starts at the end and works backwards. As the miners finish coal removal of a section and retreat outwards, they allow the mine walls and ceiling, previously held up with hydraulic props, to crumble down behind them as they pull out. This is considered safer than regular mining where one excavates as one digs deeper into the mine, having to prop up more and more of the mine as one removes increasing amounts of coal.

One mine, two systems

The two coal mines in this study were actually the same physical mine under two very different systems of ownership and management. Valley Colliery is the alias for the mine that was nationally owned and run by British Coal. Coal Co-operative refers to the mine after the miners bought it and converted it into a worker co-operative. I interviewed the miners after the conversion into a co-operative. Therefore, some of the data rely on their recollections of the organization three years earlier, when British Coal owned the mine. Although the study is somewhat dependent upon interviewees' memories, their perceptions of the differences in the company before and after the worker buy-out provide important insights regarding workers' attitudes towards raising grievances. Moreover, by studying the same company, this study avoids many comparability problems that arise from comparisons of two or more companies, such as variation in the composition of the workforce, challenges at separate work sites, and dissimilar institutional histories.

The data were drawn from 41 interviews of mine workers. Of these workers, all but three had also been at the coal mine before the worker buy-out. Each interview was open-ended and lasted about an hour, with a few interviews lasting several hours. Of these, 5 were managers, 3 were under-managers, 2 were heads of the local union lodge, 8 did surface work, 36 worked underground, 37 had worked at other mines at some point, all were white, 40 were Welsh, and 4 were women. In addition to interviews, I also gathered data from non-participant observations. I observed the control room for many hours; ate in and observed the canteen; and went one mile down into the mine to where the coal was being excavated, speaking informally to miners along the way. I also read numerous local Welsh newspaper articles about the mine, spanning a three-year period. I revisited the mine one year later, and again nine years later.

The mine was located in South Wales, which at the time had the lowest average household income and expenditure of any region in the United Kingdom. Senior citizens on social security comprised one-fifth of the population, a proportion second only to the southwest area of England. Wales had the highest rate of trade union membership in the United Kingdom at 41.6 percent of employees across all occupations. Conversely, the employment rate for men in Wales was the lowest in the UK at 65.6 percent. (For women, the rate was 49.6 percent, the second lowest, after Northern Ireland.) For those employed full-time, the average manual labor weekly gross wage for men was £284.50 and £185.40 for women. This average men's wage was second lowest after the East Midlands, although the women's wage was approximately average for the United Kingdom (Church 1996).

Valley Colliery was a Welsh coal mine that had been owned by British Coal, the government board that took over the coal industry after nationalization. In the most recent decade of government coal mine closures, 26 mines had closed in the area, leaving Valley as the only remaining deep-pit mine in Wales (Malone and Durisch 1995). In April 1994, Valley Colliery was finally closed, and the miners and other workers were given "redundancy money," large cash payments based on the duration of employment (Watson 1996). The closing of this mine would have meant the end of deep-pit mining in Wales. As part of the then-Tory government's privatization program, it was offered for private sale. Rather than remain unemployed or enter lower-paid, lower-status occupations, such as factory work, many of the workers organized to buy the mine, with approximately 200 former employees putting in £8,000 each (approximately $13,000 at the time) for the purchase price (Watson 1996). For this money, each worker received a single share worth a single vote. Some employees had enough redundancy money to buy their shares. Others had to use their savings or negotiate loans. For most of its existence, Coal Co-operative was the only worker-owned colliery in Europe (Coal Co-operative closed on January 25, 2008.).

Valley had been known for many decades as one of the more progressive and militant coal mines. For example, in the "October Revolution" of 1969, Valley Colliery was "one of the "Magnificent Seven" South Wales miners' lodges that took unofficial industrial action in support of the terribly low wages of surface workers. This action was seen as the beginning of the revival in militancy" (Francis 1997: 10). In addition to being one of the most active lodges in the 1985–86 strike, the members of Valley Colliery rallied against the closure of other area mines, against apartheid in South Africa, for the peace movement, and against factory and hospital closures throughout the United Kingdom (Francis 1997). The militancy at Valley Colliery affected dispute resolution as well. The managers, under British Coal, refused any sort of informal dispute resolution. Similarly, the unions would use formal action and grievances instead of negotiating. As one former shift head described:

> I remember days [when] I said, "Pack up your bags. We are going." And [the miners] would walk out. Then you get the next shift coming in and they don't even get under ground because there's a meeting on the top: "We're not going down if the other shift walked out." And they'd go home. They wouldn't take any messing about from anybody. You had more one-day stoppages here than anywhere else, in any other industry.

Dispute resolution in at Valley Colliery will be discussed further in Chapter 4.

Valley Colliery itself, as the last deep-pit mine in Wales, had a relatively heterogeneous workforce: as each mine closed, some miners retired, but others transferred to the remaining mines. When those mines closed, these workers transferred to whichever mines remained. Eventually, Valley Colliery was the only mine left. As a result, Valley's workforce included miners who were dedicated to the mining culture and industry, so much so that some were commuting more than an hour in order to work at the mine. Many miners believed the miners remaining at Valley Colliery were also the most militant because they did not take factory jobs or accept welfare payments, but stayed in the mining industry.

The miners were proud of the diverse nature of their workforce. A few decades earlier, each deep-pit coal mine in Wales had a small village around it and miners from that village worked exclusively in that mine. Each mine had its own culture; for example, some mines spoke Welsh and others spoke only English. As the mines began closing, miners from one village would go to work in the mine of another village. This often caused tension among the workers. However, at Valley Colliery/Coal Co-operative, the miners were from so many different villages that no one group dominated or formed a strong clique. The miner, below, spoke of how nearly all the miners began at some other mine originally:

> [Coal Co-operative] is like a United Nations, now, because it has so many people from so many different areas. But we mix not too bad; we get on pretty good. We're all foreigners. There's not many original [Valley Colliery miners], here; we all come from outside.

In this way, the success of Coal Co-operative challenges some of the assumptions about worker co-operatives, since this co-operative not only had a heterogeneous workforce, but also survived in an industry with substantial capital requirements. As Wright discusses, "[s]keptics of co-operatives argue that … worker-owned co-operatives can only effectively survive in small niches in which there is a relatively homogeneous workforce in stable markets with low capital requirements" (Wright 2010: 168).

Not all of the workers employed at Valley Colliery came back to join Coal Co-operative. Older employees, whose redundancy payments from the government were more substantial, chose retirement. Also, while all workers were invited to buy into the co-operative initially, those who hesitated too long found the mine no longer had a position for them since it accepted new members on a first-come, first-join basis.

The members of this new co-operative were not exclusively the former rank-and-file employees. By law, a mine must have certain professional managers to be in charge of specific aspects, such as safety, engineering, and finance. These managers also had to buy into the co-operative with £8,000 each, entitling each of them to a single vote.

While these managers had some significant day-to-day power over the miners, they were no longer in the position of privileged power they previously held. First, they were fewer in number; Coal Co-operative had only one-third as many managers as Valley Colliery, even though it employed approximately the same number of miners. Moreover, the board of directors (elected annually by membership) could override managers' decisions. Also, members of the co-operative had carefully chosen which managers to invite to join the co-operative; the majority were brought in from elsewhere, or had worked at the colliery previously, but only as under-managers. The managers varied in their degree of supportiveness toward co-operative ideology: one was so worker-identified that he joined the miners' union, while others saw their current position as just another job and resented the interference from the board of directors.

Thus, a minimal degree of hierarchy still remained at Coal Co-operative, even while the organization was much flatter and included fewer supervisory levels than would be present in a conventional organization. Moreover, although some positions were still arranged within a hierarchical system, no position had complete power; decisions could be overridden by the elected board and consultation with, and inputs by, the workers became the governing ideology.

Several labor unions were recognized at both Valley Colliery and Coal Co-operative; the National Union of Mineworkers (NUM) represented the vast majority of the workforce. At Coal Co-operative, the unions were still significant in the area of formal grievances. Worker-owners brought formal grievances through the union as written complaints, in the same way they had at Valley Colliery.

In the open-ended interviews I asked similar core questions, although I presented additional, tailored questions to people with unique experiences (such as managers, directors, or those on the buy-out team). Because of the open format, interviewees could, and often did, share additional information. I asked all subjects to recall problems or concerns they had experienced when British Coal ran the mine versus when it was a co-operative. Then I asked which actions they contemplated, which actions they took, what others did, and what finally happened. I also asked all interviewees to respond to a few hypothetical cases and describe what they thought would have happened under British Coal versus what would have been the outcome under co-operative management. In addition to interviews, I also gathered data from semi-participant and non-participant observations, and observed a few potential grievances.

Taxicab Companies

Taxicab driving is not a typical job; cab drivers do not occupy a single designated station, window, or office. Instead, they roam the streets continuously. In addition, their income is always uncertain: it can be affected by road conditions, generosity of passengers, skillfulness of dispatchers, personal ability, and luck. For women, especially, cab driving is not a typical occupation, yet women comprised approximately 15 percent of the drivers at both taxicab companies in this study.

One consequence of the mobile nature of cab driving is that drivers rarely deal with any one customer on an ongoing basis. This makes the job exciting, with its constant variety, and more dangerous, because of more unknowns. Potentially unpleasant situations can range from stick-ups to harassment by drunken passengers, to fare-jumpers to inadvertently harboring persons fleeing the police (Davis 1959). For these reasons, many taxicab drivers feel their occupation is dangerous and unpredictable (Onishi 1994; Wolf 1993).

Because of their location in a medium-sized, progressive Midwestern college town, not many drivers at either Co-op Cab or Private Taxi felt that they were in constant danger. The potential for trouble was never far from their minds, but few described regularly fearing for their safety. Both companies maintained radio codes that drivers could use in the event that they needed the police or other cabs to come to their immediate assistance. Everyone knew the codes and many interviewees shared one or two stories about someone actually using them. Nevertheless, nearly all the drivers emphasized that their experiences were unlike that of driving cabs in larger cities, such as New York or Chicago.

Both companies are located in a city known by the alias of Prairieville. This city, with a population of 200,000, had been ranked as the best place to live by *Money* magazine and the best city for women by *Ladies Home Journal*, with highest scores (of the top ten cities) specifically for a robust economy, a low crime rate, and an excellent education system (Langway 1997). Many drivers said they loved working in Prairieville, but would never dream of driving a cab someplace else. As one woman cab driver at Private Taxi said, "[Prairieville] is a very domestic town. The crime rate is low. The unemployment rate is low. This is the best place to drive cab – the only place I'd drive cab."

The presence of a large university affected the character of the cab companies. They are known for employing overly educated drivers, often with advanced degrees (Langway 1997). Three cab companies operated in the city: Co-op Cab, Private Taxi, and Yahoo Cab. Co-op Cab was the oldest and largest cab company in Prairieville and charged the highest rates. Private Taxi was nearly as large as Co-op Cab and about ten years younger. While Private Taxi charged slightly less than Co-op Cab, Yahoo offered much lower rates by encouraging drivers to double, triple, and quadruple fares—allowing several passengers with different destinations in the cab at once—a practice rarely allowed by the other companies. Yahoo Cab was not included in this study.

CO-OP CAB

Co-op Cab was founded in the late 1970s out of a strike and subsequent closing of two other cab companies. A handful of out-of-work cab drivers decided to try to circumvent future management-labor disputes by opening their own new cab company as a worker co-operative. Prairieville, in which Co-op Cab was located, was supportive of various alternative ways of conducting business and was the home of a number of food, housing, and producer co-operatives, as well as other smaller worker co-operatives. This support for co-operative ventures may have contributed to Co-op Cab's commercial success, despite its having the most expensive rates of Prairieville's three cab companies. Although Co-op Cab members expressed a strong commitment to democratic and co-operative ideals, economic survival—not ideology—was the primary reason for the company's creation. Founding members were first concerned with providing a living for themselves and other cab drivers; the cab strike and subsequent closings had left many drivers unemployed. Even today, although the identity of being a worker co-operative is important to the company and its members, Co-op Cab defines itself as first being a cab company, second as a co-operative.

Co-op Cab developed a formal grievance system to address discipline-related grievances, using a committee of members called the Workers' Council. When a member violated a policy or work rule, management penalized them by sending a disciplinary letter accompanied by a number of punitive points. These points affected the member's income: each point represented an additional 50 cents per shift that the member must pay for the following 50 shifts. For example, a four-point letter would mean that the member would be docked a total of $100. In addition to the immediate economic harm from acquiring points, if a member accumulated 12 or more points within a year, they could be fired. However, dismissal was neither immediate nor certain with the 12th point; a number of drivers continued to work at Co-op Cab with well over 12 points. To dispute the disciplinary letters and their accompanying points, members brought grievances before the Workers' Council. The Workers' Council was comprised of five to eight randomly chosen members who heard both sides of the dispute. The grievant could bring an advocate, often a fellow worker, who presented the case and argued on the grievant's behalf. The Workers' Council would then decide between upholding the letter and its amount of points or overturning the decision.

In addition to disputing discipline decisions, members also used the grievance system to initiate discipline against other members. For example, if one member sexually or racially harassed another member, that second member could bring a grievance before the board of directors, six people elected from the membership. This second grievance system was used less often.

I interviewed members who had brought grievances, who had sat on the grievance committee, and who had been elected to the board of directors. I included founding members, middle-term members, and new hires, who were still on probation. I spoke to drivers, dispatchers, mechanics, and managers. I also included men and women, night-shift and day-shift workers, part-time and full-time workers, and former and present members. Since some interviewees wore many hats—for example, founder, night-shift driver, dispatcher, Workers' Council member—a few interviews lasted several hours. I revisited this co-operative eleven years after the initial interviews.

PRIVATE TAXI

Private Taxi was begun in the late 1980s by two men, starting with only a few vehicles. As the company grew, one of the partners tired of the long days of dispatching, customer relations, vehicle maintenance, and occasional driving shifts. In 1990, this partner sold his half and left the taxicab business. In the 1990s, the business continued to grow, gaining more ongoing contracts for service as well as greater name recognition. At the time of this study, Private Taxi was about 75 percent of the size of Co-op Cab. Private Taxi had an owner, one manager, and a formal grievance system. In addition to managers, dispatchers at both cab companies had a minimal level of disciplinary authority over the drivers during their shifts.

Private Taxi's grievance system was a single procedure. Employees could appeal a disciplinary decision or bring a formal complaint by filling out a grievance form, available in the break room or from the manager. They would then turn the form in to the manager or the owner. If the manager received the form, they would meet with the party filing the grievance and any other parties involved and then make a decision. The manager's decision could be appealed to the owner. If the grievance was given directly to the owner—for example, if the complaint involved the manager—no appeal was available.

As I did at Co-op Cab, I interviewed a variety of people from Private Taxi, including a full spectrum of employees and the owner. I conducted some interviews at the site and others away from the Private Taxi building. I used a modified snowball method; I met more than a third of the interviewees by spending time in the break room, and then had these subjects refer me to other workers.

Whole Food Distributors

The whole food distributors in this study did not make food; they distributed organic produce or foods made from organic produce with minimal processing. Both companies in this study primarily supplied to organizations, although they both had mechanisms through which the general public could also buy directly.

The organic food distribution industry attracts a variety of people. Because food distribution demands a great deal of physical labor, many people in the industry do not have college educations or other specific qualifications. While some people take jobs in this industry simply for the salaries, others seek out such jobs for ideological reasons. These ideologically driven workers strongly believe in organic foods and want to work as part of the organics movement. Others are attracted to the industry because they feel it is more ethical than other jobs available. Workers at both the conventional and the co-operative businesses spoke of ideological motivations for holding jobs in whole foods distribution.

ORGANIX CO-OP

Organix Co-op, a major organics wholesaler, was formed in 1976 in a college town in the north of England by a handful of men, most of whom attended the same university. They formed Organix for ideological reasons; to create worthwhile jobs and a healthy atmosphere. In 1988, the co-operative sought a larger space, so it moved from the college town to a small, economically depressed town, also in the north of England. In this formerly bustling center of the wool industry, many of the town's former wool factories sat empty, their white brick exteriors stained a dirty black. Organix Co-op created its new home in one of these old factory buildings, converting the open factory spaces into a warehouse and offices.

This move changed more than Organix's physical space; it also provided Organix with a different kind of workforce. In its first home, many of Organix's workers—including its founders—were graduates of the large university in that city. These workers, white and middle-class, were drawn to Organix because they believed in or were intrigued by the idea of worker co-operatives, because they strongly believed in organic foods, or both. After the move, the demographics of the workforce began to change (although the workers already with Organix generally stayed with the co-op, either commuting or moving to the new town). Few new members were college-educated or middle-class, although these newcomers shared a dedication to organic foods and were intrigued with co-operative structure and ideology.

In fact, workers at Organix showed more zeal for worker co-operative ideology than members of any other co-operative in this study. Members of Organix enjoyed passionately discussing and critiquing co-operative theory and sharing insights into how best to apply theory to practical situations. In fact, some members had left better paying jobs to come to Organix or commuted more than an hour to remain part of the co-operative.

The level of physicality of jobs varied. Some jobs required a great deal of physical stamina and at least a modest amount of physical strength. These jobs included the order packers, shelf fillers, and truck drivers. In addition to requiring more physical exertion, these jobs were done in the warehouse, which was kept quite cold year-round, or on the road, with a range of weather conditions and traffic problems. Other jobs were less physically demanding, such as the product ordering or customer relations work. Members in these positions worked in offices that were carpeted, heated, and quite comfortable.

Unlike the other co-operatives in this study, Organix operationalized their belief in equality by paying all members the same wage, £300 gross weekly. This compensation was greater than the average full-time manual gross weekly earnings for men (£285.50) or women (£176.20) for this area of Yorkshire (Langway 1997). Yet, some members felt that people who performed certain jobs, such as heavy lifting, should be paid more to compensate for the unpleasantness of the job. Others believed that people in jobs that would command higher salaries elsewhere, such as the financial organizers, should be paid more to prevent highly skilled people from leaving.

Another egalitarian policy that evidences Organix's commitment to co-operative ideals was its decision to more evenly distribute physical work. According to the job-sharing policy, workers would share mentally demanding jobs and physically demanding positions. For example, rather than one person handling all of the buying of grains five days each week, two people alternated days and shared a desk, computer, and files. When these grain buyers weren't buying grains, they would fill orders in the warehouse, deliver goods to customers, or fill the delivery trucks.

Nearly all the workers carried out this job-sharing arrangement, although some people complained about a few men who worked in the financial office who did not participate as much as they should. These men were founders or long-time members. Members expressed their awareness of these men's positions of power (due to their knowledge of finances and their tenure) by referring to their office as the "top office." Physically, the financial office was located in a small office on the tiny floor above the other offices, but the name "top office" referred to both its location as well as to the power and authority enjoyed by those who worked in it. I asked these "top office" workers whether they shared jobs. They said they did, but only provided examples of helping "pick orders," which everyone did, as I explain below. When I asked who shared their jobs, they explained to me that no one else could and that they simply could not take the time to teach more people. One financial worker told me he could not job share, despite the fact that he had trained a woman to do enough of his work so she could fill in for him when he took long vacations (which everyone did).

In an effort to share the less-pleasant tasks, everyone was also required to help "pick orders" on occasion. Often this would happen when an order was running behind near the end of the day. In order to help everyone leave the warehouse, members would pitch in to help fill the remaining orders. If a truck was waiting to leave at the end of the day and several orders were still unfinished, someone from the warehouse would run through the office, calling out for help filling the orders. There was great pressure, at this call for help, to drop whatever they were doing, save files, pack up desks, and run down to the warehouse to help.

The high level of gender equity at Organix was a source of pride for many interviewees. Most operations had worker-managers and each area had a leader; women filled many of these positions. Each section had a representative to the Management Council, which met regularly on Wednesday afternoons. Four of the eight positions on the Management Council were reserved for women. Representatives sat for two-year, staggered terms. Some women did seem to experience a high level of power in the organization although many people pointed out that no women worked in the "top office."

Most people interviewed felt that women were nearly equal to the men at Organix—or at least more so than any other business. The concept of "nearly equal" is a divider for many of the interviews. Some people—generally men, but also some women—felt that this level of "near equality" was a great accomplishment. Others—generally women but also some men—felt that women being "nearly equal" was insufficient and that women needed to be completely equal to achieve the co-operative ideals.

In addition to the four seats reserved for women on the Management Council, the co-operative implemented other policies that were designed to encourage women's greater equality in the organization. Some policies would be proposed and implemented only to die out and then be resurrected a few years later. Two examples of these were the Women's Caucus and the childcare stipend. Both had previously been implemented and terminated at the time of the study, yet several people I interviewed mentioned current plans or attempts to revive them.

The grievance procedure at Organix included four steps: the first step was to informally approach the person, group, or part of the organization involved to try to find a solution informally. Step two was to present the grievance to the elected members of the grievance committee. Step three involved a meeting of the committee, where it would make recommendations either to the people involved or to the co-operative as a whole. Workers who presented before the grievance committee could bring an advocate or "guide" with them. The decisions the grievance committee made were reported in the management committee minutes. A grievance decision was usually widely publicized, because it affected the whole company. Finally, if the grievance committee was unable to resolve the dispute, it might refer the problem to the co-operative as a whole, with the permission of the parties involved.

All but three of the 35 interviews were conducted on site, in rooms not in use at that moment. I interviewed a variety of workers: men and women; recent hires, long-timers and founding members; warehouse workers, "top office" workers, and sales staff; white and non-white members; college-educated and those with only a secondary education; members who were raised locally, who still commuted from the college town, and who commuted from elsewhere (the farthest was North Wales); members on the management committee, grievance committee, and recruitment committee; members who had and who had not brought grievances; and former and present members. Interviews lasted from 20 minutes to several hours. I revisited this co-operative the following year after the initial interviews.

HEALTHBITE DISTRIBUTORS

I selected HealthBite for this study because it was similar to Organix Co-op in many ways, including the gender and racial balance of its workforce, the hours of operation, and the mission of the business. I found HealthBite by asking people at Organix what non-cooperative organic food distribution companies were similar to Organix. Of the two companies mentioned most often, HealthBite offered the best comparison to Organix.

HealthBite Distributors was formed when two individually owned organics wholesale businesses merged in the early 1990s. One acted as more of a wholesale warehouse store; the other served mainly as a distributor to individual homes and organizations. HealthBite was primarily a distribution company, serving the Greater London area, although individuals could come to the warehouse and buy off the skids. The two owners, now partners, shared management of the business in the new London location.

HealthBite Distributors employed a total of 32 employees. I interviewed 18 of these, including both owners. HealthBite employees earned £6 per hour and received a 20 percent discount on any food they purchased from HealthBite. This full-time weekly wage of £240 was below Greater London's average for male full-time wages for manual labor of £327.60, but above the average female wage of £226.60 (Langway 1997). Some of the employees came to HealthBite for ideological reasons, specifically because they believed in organic foods. Many of these workers viewed their work at HealthBite as part job, part vocation, especially those who dealt with sales and customers. Other organic-food-conscious employees saw their work just as a job, but took this specific job because they appreciated the employee discount and felt that the work was less "ethically stressful," as one man phrased it, than other jobs. Some employees took the job with no concern for organic foods; they just wanted a paycheck. However, a few of these employees said their appreciation for health foods grew while on the job.

The company included a medium-sized warehouse, which included one walk-in refrigerator, two sets of offices (one for the managers and one for the phone workers), and a few delivery trucks, one of which was solar-powered. The working conditions varied with the weather and the season, but were never especially pleasant. During the hot days of summer, the offices and most of the warehouse were very hot. The warehouse "loft" where small canned goods were stored, could be particularly sweltering and quite cold during the winter. As one warehouse worker said, "The staff needs better office facilities. Cleaner, more efficient, because people tend to work better in a clean place."

People also complained about the unheated bathrooms, which became uncomfortably cold in winter. The bathrooms, which were minimally lit and shared with two other businesses on the site, were located about 83 yards from the main exit of HealthBite. They also had concrete floors, which were severely uneven, creating standing puddles in snowy or rainy weather.

HealthBite's formal grievance procedure consisted of writing a letter explaining the grievance to a manager or owner. While this procedure was officially stated in the handbook, no one I interviewed knew of anyone actually bringing a formal grievance.

All 18 interviews were conducted on-site, either outdoors away from the building itself, in the warehouse of the neighboring building, or inside HealthBite, but away from other workers. The interviewees were drawn from each area of the company: phone workers, deliverers, packers, drivers, and the night workers who unloaded the shipments. Tenure of employees ranged from two months to 5 1/2 years. I interviewed 11 men and 7 women; 2 men and 1 woman identified as non-white. Both of the managers were white men. The employees' levels of education ranged from a master's degree in electronic energy to the minimum high school requirement (graduation at age 15).

Although most employees were in their late-mid 20s, the ages of employees ranged from 22 to 53 years old.

Works Cited

Church, J. (1996). *Regional Trends*. London: Government Statistical Service.

Davis, F. (1959). The Cabdriver and his Fare: Facets of a Fleeting Relationship. *American Journal Sociology* 65:158–165.

Dennis, N., Henriques, F. and Slaughter, C. (1956). *Coal is Our Life: an Analysis of a Yorkshire Mining Community*. London: Tavistock Publications.

Francis, H. (1997). *The Coal Co-operative Story: Lessons in Vigilance and Freedom*. Hirwaun: Coal Co-operative Limited.

Langway, L. (1997). The Best Cities for Women. *Ladies Home Journal*, November, 199–204.

Malone, A. and P. Durisch 1995. Buyout Miners Hit a Lucrative Seam. *The Sunday Times*. Aberdare, Wales.:10.

Onishi, N. 1994. Taxi Panel Requires Bullet-Resistant Partitions. *New York Times*. New York: B4.

Pump-House-Museum. (1997). *The World On Our Backs*. Manchester: The Pump House: People's History Museum.

Ragin, C.C. (1987). *The Comparative Method: Moving beyond Qualitative and Quantitative Strategies*. Berkeley: University of California Press.

Sunderland Museum. (1997). *Life and Work in the Coal Mining Communities of East Durham*. Sunderland: Sunderland Museum.

Watson, N. (1996). *The Involvement of Trade Unions in the U.K.: Promotion and Development of Large Co-operatives*. Wales Co-operative Centre.

Wolf, C. (1993). Massive Cabdriver Protest of 35 Killings Snarls Traffic. *New York Times* (Late New York Edition). New York: B1.

Wright, E.O. (2010). *Envisioning Real Utopias*. New York: Verso.

4

Mining the Depths of Co-ownership: The Coal Industry[1]

This chapter more thoroughly explores the workplace culture and dispute behavior at the Welsh mine, Coal Co-operative. As explained in Chapter 3, coal mines were privately owned in Britain until 1947, when the government nationalized the coal industry. British Coal, the government board, owned the mine until it closed in 1994. When the Tory government offered the mine for private sale, approximately 200 former employees each contributed £8,000 (approximately $13,000 at the time) for the purchase price. The workers chose to maintain similar union representation and the same grievance procedures they had used under British Coal, unusual decisions for a co-operative, but not surprising given the importance of unions in mining culture and history.

The members of this new co-operative included rank-and-file employees and a number of professional managers, required by law to oversee certain aspects of the mine, such as safety, engineering, and finance. The managers had to buy into the co-operative with the same amount of money as the miners. And, as discussed earlier, they had day-to-day power over the miners, but did not hold as much privilege as they had previously.

Before British Coal threatened to close the mine, few members of this co-operative had given much thought to worker co-operative ideology. However, faced with the possibilities of unemployment or low-wage, low-prestige factory jobs, the workers decided to take a gamble and buy the mine from the government.

---

1   Substantial portions of this chapter have been previously published in Confrontations and Compromise: Dispute Resolution at a Worker Co-operative Coal Mine. (2001). *Law & Social Inquiry* 26:555–596.

Overall, the workers felt the gamble was worthwhile. The miners described a wide array of ways that working at the mine had improved since the employee buy-out. The most important change the miners cited was the managing of disputes and grievances.

After reopening as a worker co-operative, all parties at Coal Co-operative handled disputes with greater flexibility and with a heightened sense of co-operation. According to the workers, they handled more disputes informally, but still raised some grievances through the formal system. This new inclination to resolve problems through informal confrontation and compromise also enabled members to raise issues that had been silenced under British Coal. Thus, while members raised more concerns after the conversion to a worker co-operative, they frequently addressed them before reaching formal grievance procedures.

Dispute Resolution Under British Coal

When British Coal owned the mine, dispute resolution was quite confrontational. This is not surprising, given that British Coal, with its rigid chain of command, myriad rules and strict procedures, was a classic example of Morrill's "mechanistic bureaucracy," which is likely to deal with problems in confrontational ways (Morrill 1995). At British Coal, the National Union of Mineworkers (NUM) usually handled problems.

The union generally resolved these issues formally, with such means as written grievances and day-long walkouts. Just as the union preferred formal means, the managers, as well, refused any on-the-spot negotiation and sent workers home, calling for a lockout if workers challenged their orders. Compromise was viewed as a sign of weakness and was rarely used.

Workers viewed management as often behaving unfairly and with great condescension toward the miners. Because of this lack of trust between workers and managers, the miners focused on individual concerns: pay, hours, specific job descriptions. Instead of operating in "group mode," as Tyler and Lind put it, they operated in "individual mode" (Tyler and Lind 2000). For example, if a problem arose in one section of the mine, workers from another section would not volunteer to assist without promises of bonuses and overtime wages.

GREATER WORKER FLEXIBILITY

The miners explained that, while grievances under British Coal formerly resulted in work stoppages, potential disputes were more often settled earlier and informally under co-operative ownership.[2] They believed the co-operative structure gave workers greater flexibility in upholding work rules. Many issues and conditions still existed that would have been formally contested under British Coal, warranting a grievance or other union action. Often at Coal Co-operative, these potential disputes did not develop into grievances. Interestingly, these potential disputes were not simply "lumped" or tolerated (Galanter 1974); they were no longer perceived as serious problems or "injurious experiences" (Felstiner, Abel, and Sarat 1980–81).

The following quote from a face worker (a miner who operates the machinery that carves out the coal face) explains how workers were more "easy-going" and willing to compromise under co-operative ownership:

> Under British Coal, if a face is supposed to have seven men on a team, and if there were only five men, well, we wouldn't work. And they'd say, "Work." And we'd say, "No!" We wouldn't work. But now we'd work undermanned. If it's at all possible, they will try to get another man to us, but if not, we work undermanned.

When I asked this miner why these attitudes had shifted, he replied, "It's ours. You know. It's ours."

Other miners also spoke about the decrease in dispute-oriented attitudes of the workers, recalling recent incidents when men worked overtime, for no additional pay, in order to resolve a problem on the mine's face. Interviewees also described voluntarily helping fellow miners in another part of the mine before a shift began in order to "catch up" that part of the mine, rather than bringing formal grievances for being made to do such work. These are examples of what Tyler and Lind (2000) would classify as an example of "group mode" behavior.

---

2   These comparisons between rates of grievances are drawn from interviewees' personal retrospective assessments. I could not gain access to actual numbers of formal grievances. Nevertheless, this does not detract from the findings. Access to numbers of formal grievances would only reflect formally raised grievances, and would not reflect increases or decreases in informal grievances nor attitudes regarding formal and informal grievance resolution. The interviewees' reports—those of both workers and managers—are very consistent and well triangulated.

The miners' responses were quite unanimous in emphasizing the powerful effect of the co-operative ownership system on attitudes. For example, the following miner explained that because the workers themselves are owners, they feel a strong disincentive to raise formal disputes, such as the stopping of work, which had happened under British Coal:

> *If British Coal couldn't have their own way, they'd send the men home. [Under co-operative ownership] the difference is if you have any disputes or anything, they settle within the union and the management. They get together and resolve them. Probably both sides have got to give in at the end of the day, but they are settled amicably and, obviously, for the best interests of both sides. All the men have a stake in the coal mine and it's in their best interest just to keep it going.*

"You have men now [who] will do things for the sake of the company," said another surface worker. "You wouldn't have it before. Prior to that it was the fat cats, if you like, or higher management would get the benefits. But now it's the workmen who get benefits as well."

Managers also echoed this change in dispute resolution. One manager who had worked under British Coal at several mines offered the example of how an order from management to do a small task outside a miner's job description could result in a walkout by an entire shift. However, at the co-operative coal mine, managers would request the task from workers, and the workers, in turn, would be more likely to help out:

> *Management would say, "Right. Get that pump underground and it has to be in that way around." And you might bring two of the boys off the face to get it down. The boys on the face, under British Coal, would say, "It's not my job. You get a fitter." And if they insist, that's it. Management would say, "Either take it down or walk out." "All right, we'll go." And off they'd go, and they'd take the rest of the face [workers] with them.*

> *But now, the management will say to the boys who are going down to the face, "This has got to go down to the face. Can you get it down there?" "Yeah, no problem." And the boys will pick it up and off they trot.*

SHARING POWER AND INFORMATION

The impacts of co-operative ideology, flattened structure, and shared ownership might not have resulted in greater flexibility if they had not also caused important changes in the approach to management. In addition to the sharing of financial ownership, members of the co-operative also shared power and information, strengthening what Tyler and Lind (2000) would describe as members' perceptions of their own standing and management's trustworthiness. As a result, workers no longer believed that formal grievances and disputes were the best ways to resolve problems.

Many members of the worker co-operative shared the belief that more widely dispersed power contributed to a greater willingness to compromise and a greater feeling of co-operation among workers and managers. As one worker put it:

> As it was before, under British Coal and the management, they seemed to distance themselves from the workforce. It was them and us. Whereas, now, we're all in it together; one big team, as such, or a family, you can say. Everything we work for today is distributed equally amongst us, and our aim is to prolong the life of the colliery as long as possible and give everybody a good salary and a living. And expand as much as we can to help the community around the colliery.

In addition to sharing power, members of the co-operative also shared information about the mine, in contrast to working under British Coal, where managers gave out no information to the workers and accepted no input about the needs of the mine. Rather, British Coal managers had asserted full power, giving orders that could not be questioned. This authority often led to grievances or even more drastic union action. Under co-operative ownership, information was shared in both directions: from managers to miners and from miners to managers. The following miner, who worked at the mine for more than a decade, describes the tremendous impact of this change:

> Information is readily available to the workforce because they're shareholders. People come in, ask their questions, and get truthful answers. That is a lot different than what it was under British Coal, because you only knew what they wanted you to know.

He went on to explain how this was accomplished:

> *The door must always be open. There's a newsletter. The unions, as much as possible, are involved to feed back to the workforce. We have the shareholders' meeting quarterly. If anything serious happens, like loss of market or some serious problem, every endeavor is made to have pit head meetings with every shift.*

More than half the interviewees cited this increase in worker knowledge about the company as a crucial reason for the greater disposition toward compromise rather than dispute. Increased understanding about the financial or industrial problems facing the mine made workers more flexible regarding their own needs and rights, and increased their perceptions of their full standing in the co-operative. This sharing of knowledge, with the subsequent strengthening of procedural justice, is essential in achieving a co-operative workplace. Russell (1985) emphasizes that this is an important hurdle in creating workplace equality.

Information flowing from workers to managers also reduced the need for formal grievances. The following quote from a chocker (a miner responsible for the wall and ceiling supports underground) describes how managers responded to knowledge the workers shared:

> *Under British Coal, they wouldn't talk with the men who are actually working the face. They would tell you how they wanted it done, no matter if it succeeded or not. As it is now, the captains meet with a manager once a week. The captains talk among themselves about the problems with the face. They turn around and say to the manager, "This is the way the men want to work this particular face at the moment." If it is a good policy, [the manager] agrees with them. If it isn't a good policy – if the manager thinks it's not a safe practice – he still won't allow them to do it.*

MANAGERS' BEHAVIOR AND LOCAL AUTONOMY

Many miners noted that the current head manager appeared to be open to workers' opinions and empowerment, in contrast to British Coal managers. Under British Coal, the miners matched the lack of respect they felt from the managers with their own lack of respect, resulting in strained relations and mutual resentment. Such strains often grew into formal grievances. In the co-operative, however, the managers were in informal contact with workers, demonstrating respect and openness. In the following quotation, a miner drew a comparison between the two organizations:

> *Today, the [head] manager will come out and talk to you. He very rarely goes through the pit without stopping and talking to everyone. Whereas before, the manager used to come down and he wouldn't talk to you. He'd probably tell somebody else who would tell you to do something. They felt they were super-human. Now at the coal mine the men have got a lot of respect for the manager, because at the end of the day, he owns as much of the coal mine as we do. We all have equal-share basis and he's in it for the same reason we are: to get the best out of the coal mine.*

The miners sometimes attribute this great openness to increased autonomy. When British Coal owned the mine, the top managers had reported to the area representatives in Cardiff, who then reported to the Coal Board in London. Several interviewees explained that Coal Co-operative could make its own decisions, set its own policies, and resolve its own disputes without having to have an outside authority approve decisions. Decisions were no longer imposed from outside, nor did officials who had little to do with the actual work of mining reap profits. The following miner explained how dispute resolution became easier in the absence of an external hierarchy:

> *All the problems and decisions, now, are made on this piece of ground here. Before, people in gray suits elsewhere—bureaucrats—would make decisions. But now, that's all done away with. All the decisions—regarding this coal mine and the men and everything else to do with it—are made here.*

This "home rule" not only gave the managers the authority to make immediate decisions without fear of reprisal or being overridden by "grey suits elsewhere," but it also seemed to give workers an empowering sense of autonomy.

INCREASED ATTENTION TO SAFETY

Despite the general shift toward more informal dispute resolution, miners still raised some formal grievances at Coal Co-operative. This was particularly true in the area of safety, where members described themselves as being less flexible than they had been under British Coal.

The coal mine had an exemplary safety program under British Coal, which many attributed to a vigilant union. But even greater strides have been made in safety since the mine's conversion to a co-operative. Coal Co-operative held a record for the lowest number of worker accidents in the United Kingdom. Members of Coal Co-operative explained that this heightened level of safety was due to higher standards and greater reluctance for taking any risks on the job. For example, one of the more senior miners explained how co-operative membership allowed managers less flexibility when it came to safety: "We all want to be happy when we retire at 55. Not arms gone, legs gone, fingers missing—and it does happen. You do something that's not safe and you could get hurt."

About a third of the miners I interviewed mentioned grievances that had been raised at the co-operative that would never have surfaced under British Coal. The miners did not all agree on whether this was a positive change: "We have it good now, but some people are never happy," one miner said. "They want something else and something else, and the company can only give you so much. You aren't happy, go somewhere else."

Another group of miners saw some of the complaints raised at the co-operative as legitimate. This electrician spoke of a seemingly minor complaint raised by co-operative members that was indicative of larger issues:

> Another thing they wanted changed when we came back as a co-operative was the toilet paper. The toilet paper [the miners used] was the old government, bloody thick paper. And the managers, under British Coal, they had the soft, bloody soft, pink paper. Silly little things, but it matters. It says, "I'm no better than that manager over there and he's no better than me."

Other complaints that interviewees said would have been quietly tolerated under British Coal, such as those regarding the food in the canteen, were given greater legitimacy within the co-operative. Rosen, Klein, and Young (1985) emphasize that such seemingly minor changes are important in providing "constant reinforcement of the ownership idea."

Transformation of Disputes

Understanding the early stages of dispute—the way a problem becomes a dispute and a dispute warrants a formal grievance—is key to understanding workplace dispute resolution. The change in how disputes at the coal mine evolved and transformed after it reopened as a worker co-operative offers important insights into the disputing process. Felstiner, Abel, and Sarat (1980–81) emphasized the importance of studying these early, pre-grievance stages in their classic article nearly two decades ago. Yet, often scholars' focus remains on the fully formed, formal dispute: "[Scholars] should pay more attention to the early stages of disputes and to the factors that determine whether naming, blaming, and claiming will occur ... because the range of behavior they encompass is greater than that involved in the later stages of disputes" (Felstiner, Abel, and Sarat 1980–81: 636). They add that the study of the emergence and transformation of disputes is important because it provides insight into "the capacity of people to respond to trouble, problems, and injustice" (Felstiner, Abel, and Sarat 1980–81: 652).

As discussed in Chapter 2, Felstiner, Abel, and Sarat describe how first an individual must perceive an experience as injurious (naming). Next, the person attributes the injury to the fault of another (blaming). The injured party reaches the third stage (claiming), when she voices the concern to the person or entity she has decided is at fault and asks for redress. The authors define a dispute as a claim that is rejected, either completely or partially (Felstiner, Abel, and Sarat 1980–81).

Under British Coal, disputes either fully developed into formal grievances or they were halted at the blaming stage, and were never voiced. In the worker co-operative, problems advanced through blaming to the claiming stage, raising the issues of concern for either formal or informal resolution. Some issues were transformed further than they would have been under British Coal: moving from blaming to claiming (pink toilet paper). Other concerns that would have evolved through claiming to become formal grievances under British Coal were resolved before being transformed into a dispute (performing work outside one's job duties). Thus, members of the co-operative transformed problems at various stages, not leaving issues unaddressed, avoided, or "lumped," as under British Coal, where unresolved and unvoiced disputes festered.

Since members of Coal Co-operative addressed most problems informally, these nascent grievances were removed from the disputing chain earlier and did not blossom into full disputes as they would have under British Coal. Such early-stage resolution does not represent mere problem-solving management, but a distinct change in how disputes were addressed. The change cannot simply be attributed to changes in management, but reflected a new attitude on the part of workers, as a result of becoming part of a co-operative.

A key question, however, is what does "becoming a co-operative" entail?

Becoming a Co-operative

The coal mine changed in three important ways when it became a co-operative: its structure became flatter, all workers owned it equally, and it adopted a co-operative ideology of shared power. It is difficult to ascertain which of these aspects had the greatest impact, since each aspect reinforced the others. The structure was flattened in response to the members' commitment to a co-operative ideology, but the flattened structure also reinforced this ideology. The co-ownership of the coal mine and the flattened structure provided objective confirmation to members that the ideology was in place, while the ideology helped maintain the importance of a flattened structure and shared ownership.

The conversion to a worker co-operative changed how workers and managers addressed potential workplace disputes, both directly and indirectly. Directly, the change to a co-operative increased democratic control, created greater worker power, decreased management power, and promoted greater support for worker opinions and input. Indirectly, the conversion enabled the coal mine to function independently, with managers no longer needing the British Coal Board to approve decisions. Also, the change to being worker owned allowed the workers to have some control over who the managers were, which resulted in placing people who were less adversarial to a co-operative ideal in managerial positions.

All of these changes resulted in greater procedural justice. This heightened perception of procedural justice moved members into "group mode" (Tyler and Lind 2000), enabling them to be more flexible and less rule oriented, allowing for greater informal dispute resolution. Because the co-operative achieved a greater sense of fairness, workers and managers were able to move away from sole reliance on the formal grievance procedures and resolve issues informally without the fear of being exploited.

Direct Effects

DEMOCRATIC CONTROL

The assurance of democratic control over the mine was extremely powerful for the new members of the co-operative. For example, members' confidence in the flatter, more democratic structure alleviated their concerns over including professional managers in the co-operative, something some miners resisted when first forming the co-operative. Ultimately, however, members of the new co-operative felt that the greater democratic control, especially the power of the elected board to veto managers' decisions, would provide them with sufficient power to prevent the managers from taking control of the co-operative. One member of the employee buy-out team said it was "awkward" at the beginning because the co-operative recruited managers from British Coal, the very entity that had closed the mine: "At the end of the day, we need them on board," he said. "We knew them, and we thought that with the structure we've got here, with the board of directors, they wouldn't be able to do too much damage to us."

GREATER WORKER POWER

The new structure, bolstered by co-operative ideology, led to increased power for workers. This change was not due to more powerful, assertive, or rights-focused workers being selected to join the company; rather, the flattened structure of the business and the employment of co-operative ideology actively encouraged it. More than a third of those interviewed mentioned the difficulties, upon reopening as a co-operative, in re-educating the membership to embrace its new power, become more assertive with the managers, and try to resolve problems as they occurred rather than bringing formal grievances through the union. In short, members of the co-operative were trying to equip workers with the self-confidence they need to participate with managers on equal terms. One head of the union local emphasized that it was hard to convince the membership to approach managers directly because they were accustomed to more adversarial dealings with the management: "In the first year, everybody was coming to the union, because they used to under British Coal. Even now you have to tell them, 'Go on, look, I understand. But go see your head of department first.'"

The high level of activism on the part of the co-operative's leaders could raise questions about whether the changes in grievance behavior at the co-operative resulted from these particular members' charisma, assertiveness, or other informal powers. While this is possible, it is unlikely that these individuals were, in fact, sufficiently powerful to cause these changes on their own. Rights cannot be realized without someone to assert them, as is well documented in the literature. However, these leaders were not so powerful that they could bring about the changes in dispute resolution practices without the initial changes in co-operative structure and ideology. The men who took on leadership roles at the co-operative were also leaders or activists in the union when British Coal owned the mine. Yet, while these men had been powerful enough to call for walkouts that halted work for days at a time, they were unable to change the dispute resolution behavior until the conversion to a worker co-operative.

DECREASED MANAGEMENT POWER

The effort to help the membership embrace its new power also involved teaching management to respect the workers' power, emphasizing that management's own power had been lessened. An elected member of the board of directors, who was also on the team to organize the worker buy-out of the mine, discussed the efforts to create a less authoritarian attitude on the part of the managers:

> Before they started, we told them, "At the end of the day, what you will have is the right to manage. But you are now not responsible to her Majesty's government, or British Coal. You are now responsible to shareholders, who are also the employees. But they will allow you to make the management decisions. But you are only one of the owners of this company. And you stand equal with everybody else."

> Then we had to educate the management positions here to sit and listen to what the individual has got to say. Rather than just say, "No, that's not good enough. You were away yesterday; I don't care whether you broke your leg or you fell off a bus or under a train, you should have been at work." That attitude is gone.

Thus, the leaders of the co-operative assisted the managers in embracing a more egalitarian ideology, reflecting the equality of all members. This change demanded a radical shift in management strategy from the authoritarian style practiced under British Coal.

The managers also spoke about their decreased power. Some felt negatively about the change in management's authority, as did this manager:

> We haven't got any power. I'll give you an example. What tends to happen is that the men want to finish early on a Friday. You know, they don't like working underground; they'll try and get out. That isn't new. Management used to have the power to crop people's wages or take disciplinary action against them. But there was this one Friday when the face chief, who was supposed to finish the work at quarter past seven came out about five/half five. That's two hours before they were supposed to. The manager decided not to pay them for those two hours. So, it developed and there were discussions between various people and it ended up that the manager was taken in front of the board of directors. And, the board of directors gave him a bollocking for letting it get out of hand in the first place. And, then they paid all the men. So, what message does that give the manager?

Other managers were more positive. The manager quoted below, who had worked at the coal mine several years before the buy-out, was transferred to another coal mine, and then brought back once the mine reopened as a co-operative. He felt that the change had improved the mine:

> There was very little feedback between manager and workforce [under British Coal]. It was almost by doctrine. "You will do!" And it has taken us some time to break that mold. It's a long, slow process. Some people have taken it very well. But there are certain factions in the pit now who say, "No, no, we will do it this way." And then, as a company, we say, "No, you don't do it that way; let's stop this process now. Let's go back, let's involve everybody else." You see, for people who worked for British Coal for 20 years, 30 years, it is very, very difficult. But our view is that three brains are better than two and four are better than three. And if you get information and advice from various parties, you haven't got to take it. But at least you get it, you weigh it.

This transition in management style was complex, and it did not happen overnight. However, in the three years between the reopening of the coal mine as a co-operative and the time of this study, the new management practices appear to have taken hold.

GREATER IDEOLOGICAL SUPPORT FOR WORKER OPINION AND INPUT

Rather than merely lecturing, the organizers of the worker buy-out and members of the board of directors worked to explain to the managers exactly how to manage co-operatively. Much of this involved emphasizing respecting workers' opinions and input, even if the managers did not truly believe in co-operative ideology themselves. The chair of the board of directors, for example, described how he had to both confront and re-educate managers:

> If [managers] stepped out of line when I had somebody in the room there, I never raised it in front of [the workers]. But immediately when that person left the room I said [to the manager], "Now you don't ever do that again. That's totally out of step. You simpled [made a fool of] that person. Now those days are gone. You don't step on anyone in this office anymore.
>
> On one occasion, the manager went overboard and said to this guy—34 years of age, family man—"You're just useless. You know, you're a waste of time. I don't even know why you're employed here. If it was up to me, you'd be down the road; I'd never give you a job again!"
>
> So I didn't interfere and then [the manager] finished his speech. And then I spoke [to the miner], "In my opinion, a mistake has been made here, but I'm totally confident that you will learn from this, and you will be a better person for this as of tomorrow, and as far as I'm concerned, I've seen nothing in this meeting that puts your future here at the coal mine under threat." [The miner] left and then I said to [the manager], "Don't you ever simple anybody like that again."

Managers also spoke about their struggle to learn a new way of managing after the coal mine reopened as a worker co-operative, as this surface manager explained:

> When we first started, we had one manager who used to talk to the men like dirt. He got called in for that, and after that for a couple of weeks he is a lot easier going. Not in the sense that he doesn't get the work done with the men. If anybody does anything wrong he still balls them out, but he doesn't talk to them like a piece of dirt anymore. Now he'll talk to the men, which he wouldn't do before. So in all, everybody has settled down, come to realize it's their own company. Men aren't prepared to take it anymore as they used to under British Coal.

Rosen, Klein, and Young (1985: 10) view this type of change in company culture as vital for ownership to become a "constantly renewed process, rather than a discrete event that happen[ed]."

Indirect Effects

INDEPENDENT, AUTONOMOUS MINE

Just as the managers had less authority over the workers, the managers themselves became more autonomous after the mine became a co-operative. The managers answered to the coal mine's board of directors, not the entire bureaucratic hierarchy of British Coal. Managers and workers spoke about the impact of no longer being under British Coal's supervision. The manager quoted below believed that the increased autonomy allowed managers to focus on important issues rather than wasting time to report back to area and national-level supervisors:

> There was a hierarchy above each individual coal mine ... I'd say that 30 percent to 35 percent of my time was spent satisfying those people. We would never pick up the phone to ask them [Headquarters] for help. They would always pick up their phone asking us for information. But you'd give them the information and they'd just give you a bollocking and tell you to sort it out. That's all been removed, so we concentrate on things that are important to us. We can tailor whatever we want to do to the needs of the coal mine.

This greater autonomy of the mine was an important indirect effect of the conversion to a worker co-operative that facilitated the new grievance behavior. The board chair explained that the removal of the threats from local and national headquarters' oversight allowed managers to work within the goals of the co-operative ideology:

> The management said to me recently that what surprised them the most about the company now is that they can actually admit to mistakes without the worry of being sacked or sent to another pit. And they found that the most helpful of all – working without the threat of being sacked when you make mistakes.

While the removal of the hierarchy above the mine helped create an atmosphere where change was possible, the absence of British Coal alone was insufficient to create the changes in dispute resolution behavior found at Coal Co-operative. As the conventional businesses in the other two industries discussed in this book demonstrate, merely making a business autonomous does not produce the type of dispute resolution behavior found at Coal Co-operative. While the autonomy of the coal mine was important in that it allowed the management to run the mine as it wished, the direction that it chose to take was far more significant in changing dispute resolution practices. This direction was more affected by the re-establishment of the mine as a co-operative, while the mine's autonomy merely allowed the mine and its management to have this choice.

WORKERS ALLOWED SOME CONTROL OVER HIRING MANAGERS

The second indirect effect of being co-operatively owned was that the workers had some control over who the managers were, and thus, could avoid hiring managers who would be the most adversarial to a co-operative ideology. This did not mean, however, that the mine was able to hire managers who strongly favored a co-operative ideology; they were simply able to avoid the most oppositional managers. Because the pool of potential managers was severely constricted by law and general availability, the hiring process rarely resulted in the selection of managers who were pro-cooperative or even pro-worker. For example, this member of the interview team explained how they selected managers first for their abilities: "We got the safety engineer who's the finest in the country, and the mechanical engineer from British Coal, who was not far off the best," he said.

However, the committee hired three managers because they were thought to be more open to co-operative ideology: "Some of the ones who are managers now, they were here as under-manager, or some of us had worked with them. We knew they were in favor of the buyout," one miner explained.

The members of Coal Co-operative deliberately hired some managers from outside the coal mine. Although these managers were not necessarily supporters of a co-operative ideology, their distance, as outsiders, from the bad feelings around the closing of the mine was seen as helpful. For example, one director explained how the manager of the electrical engineers wasn't a part of the mine's closing: 'Since he wasn't here then, there's not so many bad feelings between the work force and him.'

Members of the co-operative viewed several managers as hostile and opposed to co-operative ideals, but hired them, nonetheless, because their jobs had to be filled and they were seen as no worse than the alternatives. For example, the hiring committee interviewed nearly 50 accountants before settling for a financial manager who was not particularly supportive of co-operative ideals.

Similarly, because the safety manager was resistant to the co-operative changes, some members still disliked him, despite his technical expertise. Nevertheless, all but one person who commented on him said he was as good a choice as any for the job, echoing this miner's sentiment: "The manager is the same manager that we had under British Coal. He was the under-manager under British Coal. But we took him on as our manager. He's still the same, but what the hell. As long as he does his job, everything's all right."

While the process of choosing managers did allow the membership to prevent the worst managers from joining, it did not result in a pro-cooperative or even consistently accommodating management team. Indeed, much of the re-education of the management after the conversion to a co-operative, discussed earlier, would not have been necessary if the co-operative had hired only pro-worker managers who supported the conversion. Nevertheless, even the managers who were not initially in favor of the new system accepted it and adapted to a new, more informal style of negotiating and managing. This shift implies that strategic hiring helped the co-operative to avoid the managers who were most adamantly opposed to a worker co-operative.

Conclusions

This chapter has examined the effect of workplace hierarchy, employee ownership, and worker empowerment on dispute resolution at Coal Co-operative. As in the other industries, the members of the co-operative enjoyed more dispute resolution options than workers in a conventionally organized mine. After the coal mine reopened as a co-operative, the miners were more likely to raise concerns, but less likely to resolve them through formal action. Informal negotiation and compromise became the preferred ways to address most problems. This change in the company's dispute resolution behavior is explained by several key changes in the ways the workers and managers approached potential disputes.

First, both managers and workers were more willing to compromise. Rather than giving orders, managers would consult with workers and make decisions that incorporated worker input. Rather than forbidding questioning, co-operative managers accepted negotiation with workers as integral to managing a worker co-operative. Similarly, many issues that would previously have been dealt with formally through union action were now negotiated informally. For example, workers no longer strictly adhered to the official rules regarding how many workers must be on each team. So long as no work team was grossly understaffed, the workers often perceived the potential harm to the co-operative posed by a work stoppage as overriding the working conditions created when a team was short a worker or two.

Furthermore, some concerns that workers would have raised as grievances were no longer perceived as problems. For example, shifts' ending times were less rigorously maintained, with employees willing to work overtime in order to complete tasks necessary for the mining to move forward. Under British Coal, employees never worked overtime without full compensation. At Coal Co-operative, the focus was on the company as a whole, and less on individual circumstances. Thus, situations that occurred under British Coal — such as the need to work overtime without overtime pay — still occurred, yet were no longer perceived as problems; hence they no longer necessitated formal grievances. Applying the categories of Felstiner, Abel, and Sarat (1980–81) to this example, unpaid overtime was no longer perceived as an injurious experience because it helped the co-operative as a whole.

Paradoxically, workers at Coal Co-operative felt able to raise some issues that had been diminished — or not mentioned due to fear of retribution — under British Coal. The change in toilet paper, for example, had great morale implications, but would never have been taken seriously under British Coal. Now, it had the status of a legitimate dispute.

Additionally, some members of the co-operative continued to formally raise concerns that they had under British Coal. According to the miners, the vast majority of formal grievances raised at the co-operative concerned safety issues.

Works Cited

Felstiner, W.L.F., Abel, R.L. and Sarat, A. (1980–81). The Emergence and Transformation of Disputes: Naming, Blaming, Claiming … *Law and Society Review* 15:631–654.

Galanter, M. (1974). Why the 'Haves' Come Out Ahead: Speculations on the Limits of Legal Change. *Law & Society Review* 9:95–127.

Morrill, C. (1995). *The Executive Way*. Chicago: University of Chicago Press.

Rosen, C.M., Klein, K.K. and Young, K.M. (1985). *Employee Ownership in America: The Equity Solution*. Lexington, Massachusetts: Lexington Books.

Russell, R. (1985). *Sharing Ownership in the Workplace*. Albany, N.Y.: State University of New York Press.

Tyler, T.R. and Lind, E.A. (2000). Procedural Justice. pp. 65–92 in *Handbook of Justice Research in Law*, edited by J. Sanders and V.L. Hamilton. New York: Kluwer Academic/Plenum Publishers.

5

Legal Consciousness on the Road: The Taxicab Industry[1]

This chapter turns to a very different industry: taxicab driving. Here, I compare a privately owned company, Private Taxi, and a worker co-operative, Co-op Cab. As explained in Chapter 3, both companies operated in a medium-sized Midwestern city with a low crime rate and excellent quality-of-life ratings. Co-op Cab was the oldest operating cab company in Prairieville and charged the highest rates. Private Taxi was ten years younger and nearly as large as the co-operative.

The workers at the two cab companies had somewhat different approaches to workplace disputes. The legal consciousness—the orientation toward laws and rules—within each company dictated which options the workers viewed as available and appropriate.

As discussed earlier, when faced with interpersonal problems, workers could learn to tolerate the offending behavior, leave the company, use formal grievance procedures, or engage in various forms of informal dispute resolution. Informal dispute resolution included talking to the co-worker or manager with whom one has a problem; aggressive confrontation with the person with whom one has a complaint; and seeking unofficial assistance from a manager, owner, or member of the board.

Employees at Private Taxi used only three of these four approaches: toleration, informal dispute resolution, and resignation. Members of Co-op Cab engaged in toleration, formal grievance resolution, and informal dispute

---

1   Small portions of this chapter have been previously published in Legal Consciousness and Dispute Resolution: Different Disputing Behavior at Two Similar Taxicab Companies. (2003) *Law & Social Inquiry* 28:691–715; and Dispute Resolution in a Worker Co-operative: Formal Procedures and Procedural Justice. (2005). *Law & Society Review* 39:51–82.

resolution. And while workers at both companies claimed to use informal dispute resolution, the two companies' workers differed in how they resolved disputes informally. Private Taxi workers said they spoke with co-workers with whom they had disputes, aggressively confronted them, and petitioned managers for help. In contrast, Co-op Cab members did speak with troublesome co-workers and sought help from managers, but did not turn to confrontation, either individually or collectively.

Dispute Resolution at Private Taxi

The employees at Private Taxi discussed tolerating problems, resigning their positions, or engaging in informal resolution, which included self-help, individual or group confrontation, or talking with the manager or owner. The workers at Private taxi never mentioned formal grievance resolution unless I asked them directly. When I did so, few employees anticipated using the formal grievance process: some felt it would not be effective; some simply didn't like the concept of formal grievances; and some did not even know the option for filing formal grievances existed.

TOLERATION

When I asked employees about problems at work, they frequently voiced the credo that they couldn't let themselves get upset and that "lumping it" was often the best strategy. They described cab drivers as people who were able to roll with the punches and resist becoming irritated over problems: "You usually can't let stuff like that get to you. It can ruin your whole day really fast," said one driver. "If you let one thing irritate you right at the beginning of the day: that's it! Because most likely you're dealing with the traffic anyway, and sometimes you're dealing with jerks. You just can't let it get to you."

Many drivers said they believed in controlling their anger in response to misbehavior by passengers or co-workers. They explained that cab drivers came to work to make money, not to get angry. They emphasized that the two activities were at odds, so money had to be the priority. Thus, "lumping it" became a financially important skill.

RESIGNATION

Thirty-six percent of Private Taxi drivers mentioned the option of leaving their jobs (as opposed to only 20 percent of those interviewed at Co-op Cab). Even drivers who had been at Private Taxi for many years expressed a willingness to leave: "The ultimate thing is, we can always quit," said a driver who had been with the company for more than seven years. "It's a nice job, but it's just a job. It's just cab driving."

While the limited training needed for cab driving made drivers somewhat replaceable, the low unemployment rate in Prairieville contributed to the belief by both drivers and the owner that a good driver might not be easily replaced: this gave the threat of leaving more power than it might have had otherwise.

INFORMAL DISPUTE RESOLUTION

Despite drivers' abilities to tolerate negative circumstances, problems did occur that moved them to action. When Private Taxi employees could no longer tolerate unpleasant situations, they could resolve their issues informally or they could resign. To resolve their problems informally, they could talk with the offending party, employ individual or group confrontation, or speak to a superior.

Drivers at Private Taxi often discussed ways they tried to resolve problems by themselves (conciliation). This self-help strategy sometimes involved simply talking to the other party. When discussing this strategy, interviewees sometimes characterized themselves as taking the "friendly way" or being "nice guy(s)." "You can either be confrontational about it, or you can try to be a nice guy," explained one driver. "I'm a type of guy that would rather talk through it first."

Like this driver, many Private Taxi workers expressed pride in their ability to resolve problems informally, without any formal or informal managerial action and without any aggressive confrontation. Some even described a failure to resolve problems by talking face-to-face with the other party as a failure of their personal skill and integrity. For example, the following driver said he believed in the value of talking through problems:

> *Anyone can get nasty. Little kids can act out to get their way. Anyone can. It takes effort to work things out, but that's the thing to do. You can't go getting angry all the time. You have to learn to talk and work out your problems. It's hard; you don't always want to, but that's what you've got to do.*

However, others employees at Private Taxi favored confrontation as a means of dispute resolution. Although these more hostile actions were sometimes used only as a last resort, other times they would be the only actions taken, especially if previous problems had not been satisfactorily resolved through "nicer" means.

CONFRONTATION

Confrontations were retaliatory actions taken against an offending party, either one-on-one or by a group. Most Private Taxi employees I interviewed mentioned having been involved in workplace confrontations. One-on-one confrontations included face-to-face arguments or shouting matches, which sometimes escalated to more vindictive behavior. For example, one driver who had been with Private Taxi for several years described an incident where his co-worker mistakenly thought he had stolen a call earlier in the day. When the driver came back to the company parking lot after his shift, he saw the co-worker kicking the side of his personal car, trying to dent it.

Nearly all Private Taxi drivers also described instances of group retaliation. These actions often stemmed from occasions where one driver would engage in unacceptable behavior, such as stealing calls from other drivers. In response, the other drivers would team up to take the offending driver's calls, leaving him with little income for that day. The following driver described this group retaliation technique:

> *You're not supposed to steal other people's calls. There're not really rules about that. But there's sort of an etiquette: you just want to be fair to everyone. If you start stealing people's calls, then everyone will get mad. Then everyone else will start stealing all your calls.*

> *We did this to someone a couple weeks ago who was being a real problem. We decided for a night we were going to steal every one of this person's calls. At the end of the night he'd made $20 in ten hours. He was broke, right? You just sort of do things like that; sort of teach him a lesson.*

A number of other employees at Private Taxi shared this driver's belief that this form of group action was both effective and justifiable.

PETITION OF SUPERVISOR

The third type of informal dispute resolution used by drivers at Private Taxi was to petition a supervisor for help in dealing with a problem. Drivers at Private Taxi mentioned speaking with a manager, a dispatcher, or an owner. Although many Private Taxi drivers considered talking to the manager or the owner about problems, few were consistently confident that this path would resolve the issues. People at Private Taxi emphasized the fickleness of management, in that the level of assistance often depended on whether one had developed a more personal relationship with the manager or the owner. For example, this driver, who had driven for Private Taxi for three years, explained that employees would try whatever means they could to resolve disputes informally:

> *If someone has a good relationship with [the owner], then they'll probably go to him and see what they can do. If someone has a good relationship with [the manager], at this point in time, they'll go to him to see what they can do. In some cases, people will go to the dispatcher and say, "Hey, you know, listen, I got this problem."*

In the interviews, I found that some drivers did not think Private Taxi's owner was helpful in resolving disputes, and preferred to deal with the manager. Others, who had a better relationship with the owner, chose to work through him. As a result, each employee at Private Taxi had to negotiate on his or her own, seeking informal resolution without predictable outcomes. Often, this dynamic led many employees to simply learn to tolerate problems, rather than attempting either formal or informal resolution, as discussed later.

In some instances, these conferences would resolve the problems at hand; other times they were merely the first attempt to resolve a problem before engaging in aggressive self-help. Still other times, discussions with management were the sole, unsuccessful attempt to solve the problem before an employee quit the company. The following employee explains how Private Taxi drivers were employed at the pleasure of the owner:

This is a business. This is not a democratic thing that's going on. The fact is, he owns the business and he has the right to make decisions. And if you don't like the decisions he makes, then you either swallow it or get a different job. That's just the way it is.

This driver echoed the widely held opinion at Private Taxi that people should either learn to deal with their problems or leave the company ("like it, lump it, or leave").

Thus, employees at Private Taxi had developed several means of dealing with workplace problems. Most workers learned strategies to tolerate problems. When faced with conflicts, some people talked with the offending party, aggressively confronted the offending party, or engaged the help of a manager as means of informal dispute resolution. Other times they simply quit, leaving the job and the problems behind. Although a formal grievance procedure did exist at Private Taxi, it was rarely used and often forgotten by the employees.

Dispute Resolution at Co-op Cab

In contrast to Private Taxi employees, the Co-op Cab members I interviewed consistently mentioned formal grievance resolution. In addition, few members of Co-op Cab mentioned the possibility of quitting to escape workplace problems and no one mentioned planned confrontation by an individual or by a group.

TOLERATION

Like the workers at Private Taxi, members of Co-op Cab would sometimes choose not to resolve certain problems and would rely, instead, on their abilities to tolerate unpleasant circumstances. Co-operative members commonly described tolerating disruptive passengers, who provided necessary income. And some members practiced toleration in regard to problems within the company itself. For example, this young woman driver described how she decided not to take any action against a dispatcher she felt had sexually harassed her:

One of the old dispatchers, he tends to use a lot of raunchy humor and he says certain things that could be taken definitely as sexual

> *harassment. But I choose to not look at it that way, because I think he's also extremely fair as a dispatcher, and he would never do anything to mess up my personal income. Because I happen to be a woman, he would never give me a worse call.*

In this situation, the driver prioritized her personal income over her personal comfort level. Although this dispatcher made her feel uncomfortable, she preferred not to say anything because his behavior did not affect her ability to earn money.

A distinct gender pattern emerged among the members of Co-op Cab when it came to resolving grievances. Both men and women anticipated times when they would not raise formal grievances. However, in situations in which they would not raise formal grievances, men believed they had the option of informal resolution, while women felt they could only decide whether to act formally or not act at all. For example, this cab driver explained that she primarily had two dispute resolution strategies: raise a formal grievance or learn to tolerate the situation.

> *If something is serious enough, if it's bad enough, fine. Then I'll go ahead and bring a grievance. But it if it's not, then I'm not going to go there. You have to choose what you're going to fight. The formal procedure is there and that's important. But if you don't want to put your energy there, then you have to learn to not let whatever [is the problem] get to you.*

She, like the other women cab drivers in this study, relied on their ability to tolerate problematic situations (i.e., Galanter's "lumping it" [1974]) or they would invest their time and effort into bringing a formal grievance.

The men at Co-op Cab, however, rarely mentioned toleration as a strategy. Instead, the men debated between whether to raise a formal grievance or to informally resolve the problems. For them, they had a choice between formality and informality. If they did not wish to bring a formal grievance, they could still resolve their disputes.

The "just-talk-to-the-guy" strategy is only available, however, to workers who are comfortable approaching supervisors. At Co-op Cab, female members did not feel this option was available to them, so they relied more on formal grievances.

FORMAL GRIEVANCES

Nearly all members said that they would be more likely to bring a formal grievance at Co-op Cab than at other places where they had worked; however, women were more likely to prefer formal grievances to informal processes. One cab driver, for example, expressed her belief that using the grievance process is an important aspect of co-operative membership, a belief shared by the majority of members of Co-op Cab:

> People use [the grievance procedures] if they have an issue they feel is important. Part of being in a co-operative—being a member and an owner—is being willing to bring a grievance if there's a problem. In a sense, this is both a privilege and a duty. You have to speak up and not be afraid to speak up and go to the Workers' Council.

The most common reason Co-op Cab members cited for bringing grievances was unfair treatment, either by a manager or a co-worker. Many women felt that filing a grievance was the best way to respond to unfair treatment.

When men described their hesitancy to use the formal grievance procedures, they often expressed the importance of being completely blameless before raising a formal grievance. This veteran male driver described a winter accident that resulted in a disciplinary letter:

> Yeah, I had an accident once when it was really icy that was considered my fault. It wasn't totally my fault, but I got three points. I considered debating that, but in the end that was the right decision actually, because it was my fault.

This driver was unwilling to engage in blaming, much less claiming, unless he was blameless. Yet, some women at Co-op Cab brought formal grievances, even when culpability might be partially shared. For example, one night-shift driver described an incident when another woman driver had been fired.

> Management tried to get rid of a woman who was working in our office... They fired her based on an evaluation that was arbitrary... It went to the Workers' Council... In the end, she won.

Although this woman had been fired—unjustly it would seem—she had been able to achieve a measure of justice by appealing that management decision to the Workers' Council. These recollections validated this driver's belief that the formal grievance process was often a good route for achieving justice.

Although most Co-op Cab workers said they would consider bringing a formal grievance, some members, particularly men, still preferred to resolve disputes informally.

INFORMAL DISPUTES

Like workers at Private Taxi, members of Co-op Cab resolved many disputes informally, but Co-op Cab workers employed fewer types of informal resolution than members of Private Taxi. Co-op Cab workers spoke of conciliation with offending parties and of assistance from supervisors, but they did not engage in individual or group confrontation, nor did they mention resignation as a way to resolve disputes. Moreover, men, much more so than women, favored informal resolution. The men I interviewed felt that the co-operative's informality permitted problems between co-workers and managers, or among co-workers, to be addressed more easily without raising formal grievances.

CONCILIATION

While the members of Co-op Cab felt empowered to bring formal grievances, over half of them believed they could resolve disputes as well or better through informal resolution. These workers felt they could avoid formal grievances through skillful discussions. Men at the cab company were more likely to believe this than were their women co-workers. The following quote is from a man who had worked at Co-op Cab for six years and had never used the formal grievance procedure:

> I guess my first priority, interpersonally, if I had a problem with another employee, would be to work it out with them. If I couldn't work it out with them I would be in a new kind of situation. I've usually been able to work it out.

This attitude contrasted with the feeling of many women at Co-op Cab, who did not feel that informal routes were available to them. Much of this dynamic is due to the somewhat sex-segregated socializing at the cab co-operative and the fact that most of the worker-managers, who had the power to informally negotiate grievances, were men. This created an environment in which the women lacked the social networks to enable them to resolve disputes informally (Hoffmann 2004; Hoffmann 2005).

Nevertheless, some women did anticipate resolving disputes informally, such as this cab driver, who also served on the board of directors. She provided the following example of first trying to talk to the offending party:

> *When I first started driving cab, one night I pulled a really, really, really stupid driving move. I did something really dumb with a cab full of screaming people. Another driver saw me do it. Now he could have gone running to the boss and said, "I saw so and so doing such and such." No! He tracked me down, which entailed him losing income to do that because he could have been getting another fare. He said, "Look, I just want to say, do you know what you did?" I was so embarrassed. He basically said, "Okay, look, rookie: from one driver to another, this is the drill. And you gotta learn to deal with this, otherwise somebody's gonna get hurt, and I don't want to see you get hurt." I like that. If I'm doing my job badly, I want to be told. I don't want to lose my job over it, but I don't want people saying it behind my back either.*

PETITION OF SUPERVISOR

Others members of Co-op Cab emphasized that they could easily go to managers with complaints. These workers explained that, because Co-op Cab was a worker co-operative, managers were just co-workers who could be approached without trepidation.

Such easy informal dispute resolution was a viable strategy only for those workers who had developed informal networks with those workers with the greater power. In the case of Co-op Cab, the workers who wielded more power over other workers were the worker-managers, who could discipline their co-workers, and the dispatchers, who assigned calls, affecting a drivers' work load and income. Only when drivers and worker-managers or dispatchers shared the same social circles could the drivers informally resolve their disputes. Thus, only "insiders" enjoyed the additional strategy of informal dispute resolution.

In the case of Co-op Cab, only men comprised this "insider" group. (This is discussed further in Chapter 7.) At Co-op Cab, most socializing was sex-segregated. Since nearly all worker-managers and dispatchers were men, this meant that women drivers did not socialize with the worker-managers and dispatchers, and, thus, remained outside these critical networks. In contrast, men drivers could establish social ties with these co-workers with greater power, and so could avail themselves of the opportunities to informally resolve disputes.. This man, who had been a driver several years, said:

> [Co-op Cab] is like a family, a big family. Drivers live with other drivers. I used to live with [driver] and [worker-manager]. We all go out drinking after our shifts. We even go on vacations together.

Part of this driver's pride in his membership in a worker co-operative was that he saw his manager as his friend, rather than as his oppressor, as he had at his earlier jobs. His reference to inclusion in a family also underscores a theme that some men mentioned: that their "insider" status permitted them the option of informal dispute resolution, but also somewhat discouraged them from using the formal grievance procedures. On an informal level, the men at Co-op Cab were confident of the trust, neutrality, and standing they had and so felt assured that they could informally receive justice. An aspect of this inclusion, however, was that they were inhibited from bringing formal grievances. As insiders, the men interpreted use of the formal procedures as demonstrating that they, themselves, had failed or that the co-operative had failed to work properly.

Many of the women at Co-op Cab believed that the greater familiarity between male workers and male managers not only gave men an edge with the managers, but also placed women at a disadvantage, as this woman articulated:

> [Unconscious discrimination was] why I was put back on probation when I came back. [The Worker-manager] went according to policy and put me back on probation. Since I was a woman and we weren't really buddy-buddy, he wouldn't have felt really comfortable not going according to procedure.

While both men and women members were proud of their membership in the co-operative, the women did not experience the informal inclusiveness, such as the feeling of being "a family" that the male driver described. Importantly, although both men and women were members of the co-operative, only men had the informal standing to participate in the social networks with other men, including the managers and dispatchers.

Few Co-op Cab men or women mentioned resignation as a way to handle workplace disputes. Not only did a smaller percentage of workers at Co-op Cab discuss exiting, but when they did, they did not embrace a "we-can-always-quit" approach in the way their counterparts at Private Taxi did. Also, Co-op Cab workers rarely cited quitting as a way to address workplace problems, but only mentioned leaving as an unplanned possibility of the future.

Discussion

Although Private Taxi and Co-op Cab were similar in many ways, their workers demonstrated different characteristics of legal consciousness. Both Private Taxi and Co-op Cab had supervisors and dispatchers, and both had formal channels to raise grievances. Yet, the members at Co-op Cab, particularly the women, were much more willing to bring formal grievances than their counterparts at Private Taxi. Even men, who had the easier option of informal dispute resolution, felt that formal grievances were always an option for them.

The men's hesitance to use the formal grievance procedures does not mean that they regarded the formal process as unimportant. Often, men at Co-op Cab mentioned pride in this democratic aspect of the co-operative. For these men, the formal grievance procedures provided more symbolic value than instrumental, in that these procedures acquired an "immediate intrinsic significance … a gesture important in itself" (Gusfield 1967: 181). However, for women the formal grievance procedures held instrumental importance because their actual use had a direct influence on how women approached grievances.

Drivers at Private Taxi were more likely to talk about toleration, group confrontation, or resignation than were drivers at Co-op Cab. The two companies had vastly different grievance cultures. Co-op Cab placed great emphasis on educating members about the options of the formal grievance system and on encouraging them to use the grievance system. Alternatively, Private Taxi's grievance culture emphasized handling conflicts "on one's own" and developing a self-sufficiency that steered workers away from using formal grievances.

The legal consciousness within the grievance culture of Private Taxi also varied from that of Co-op Cab in how workers anticipated resolving disputes and which strategies they saw as yielding the greatest satisfaction. Unlike their counterparts at Private Taxi, Co-op Cab workers often spoke about the importance of having a formal grievance procedure. When contrasting the cab company to previous places they worked, Co-op Cab members said that they would have felt forced to quit at other companies if they faced certain conflicts, but, at the co-operative, they could take action and resolve problems through formal grievances or informal dispute resolution.

Many workers at Co-op Cab seemed grateful to have the grievance procedures in place. For example, one woman said she had to quit a previous job because of a number of issues: "I've had wages illegally withheld, where I've not been paid overtime," she said, "I've been sexually harassed, a lot of the general gamut of experiences for women in low-wage jobs." None of her previous employers had grievance procedures.

While exiting other jobs often seemed like the only solution for workplace troubles, members of Co-op Cab said they were much more likely to resolve problems through the grievance procedures, as this phone answerer explained: "I think I would be more likely to bring a grievance and a lot more likely to be more assertive about it. I think I would just quit another job."

In contrast to the "like it, lump it, or leave" mentality of other jobs, including Private Taxi, this driver, who had been at Co-op Cab for a little more than a year, described her attitude:

> If I felt somehow that I had been unfairly disciplined, I wouldn't hesitate to appeal because I know that's what [the grievance procedure] is there for, to hear what I have to say. I would probably, right away, talk to one of the stewards. I think that's pretty much what people do when they think, on whatever level, they've been treated unfairly—by another co-op member, or by management, or by somebody on the board.

These statements contrast with those from Private Taxi workers, whose grievance culture greatly de-emphasized the formal grievance procedures, nearly removing this option from workers' legal consciousness.

Nevertheless, both companies did have grievance procedures. Yet the existence of these procedures was not in itself sufficient for the kind of legal consciousness found at Co-op Cab. In addition to having these procedures, Co-op Cab also fostered a culture that taught its members that bringing grievances was acceptable and appropriate action. Nearly everyone—both men and women—spoke of feeling encouraged to raise grievances.

The legal consciousness that existed among Co-op Cab's members did not occur passively or by chance. Organized, more senior members made deliberate efforts to teach members that they had certain rights (such as the right to use grievance procedures) and to convince them to use them. In the quote below, a member of the board of directors described the training of new members:

> When people come off probation, the head training co-ordinator gives instruction on what a co-operative is and how it works and if they have a grievance and what all that means, what corporate structure possibilities there are, how this one's different from those, and what that means. I'm kind of hoping that that will make people who are coming in—who aren't from a union shop background or a co-operative background—get the idea that if they don't like something they don't have to put up with it just because they like their job. There is probably a reason why they don't like it and it could be fixed.

Another driver described the company's efforts to specifically educate members that harassment would not be tolerated and that anyone who is harassed should take action against it.

> You'll notice right on the title page is this policy on harassment. When we do orientation for new drivers, one of the first things we tell them is, "We follow this [policy]. If you have any problems, do something about it. Don't suffer in silence; don't put up with it." I think that's part of the reason the message sinks in.

Special education efforts, including posted lists of formal grievance advocates, were necessary because many new members did not have experience asserting their workplace rights. Many workers came from other jobs where they perceived few, if any, options when they encountered problems at work. Therefore, without explicit articulation of their rights and instruction on the available procedures, members might endure many problems unnecessarily

Although not every worker at Co-op Cab had personally brought formal grievances, the formal grievance procedures held important symbolic meaning to members. More than two-thirds of Co-op Cab's members believed that the grievance procedures and rights consciousness were essential elements of their identities as members of a worker co-operative: an egalitarian, less hierarchical, pro-worker business. According to this driver, a member for more than ten years, the grievance procedures helped individuals and the organization as a whole:

> *I don't think people come in understanding that they can speak their minds without being retaliated against. [Elsewhere] if you have a big problem with your boss at work, you might go and try and hint at it. If they don't do anything, well, they're the boss. In a co-operative, if someone is having a problem, probably other people are having that problem and there could be good reasons why they're having that problem. And correcting it could increase our efficiency [as an organization]. I think people don't come in thinking that way. I think they come in thinking, "Well, the boss wants to do it that way. It's my job. I'll just do it and go home."*

In contrast, while Co-op Cab members focused on the democratic principles behind the company's co-operative ideology, Private Taxi workers emphasized the autocratic management at Private Taxi. This rights-focused culture at Co-op Cab is a dramatic contrast to Private Taxi's grievance culture, which encouraged "lumping it" and informal dispute resolution. Formal grievances were so unpopular at Private Taxi that some employees did not even know that a formal grievance procedure existed. Of those who knew the company had a grievance procedure available, none had ever brought a grievance nor did they know of anyone ever doing so.

However, Private Taxi workers did view group retaliation as appropriate, in contrast to their counterparts at Co-op Cab. Although arguments and occasional one-on-one physical fights did occur at Co-op Cab, no one mentioned group retaliation in their interviews. The irony of this situation is that the only spontaneous group action took place within Private Taxi, the company that did not actively encourage collective action. But drivers at Private Taxi demonstrated spontaneous collective actions of group retaliation, whereas the members of Co-op Cab had many established means of collective action, including committee meetings, board elections, and membership meetings. All of these could be used as forums for informal dispute resolution.

Conclusions

This chapter has explored how a co-operative and a conventional taxicab company addressed workplace disputes. Although these businesses were similar in some ways, each responded with very different displays of legal consciousness. Employees of the privately owned, hierarchically organized taxicab company, Private Taxi, rarely brought formal grievances, but instead tolerated their problems, resigned, or tried to informally resolve them through peaceful discussion, aggressive confrontation, or petition to supervisors. In contrast, members of the co-operative cab company were much more likely to bring formal grievances. If formal means were not appropriate, they resolved problems informally by speaking with a supervisor or co-worker or, less often, simply tolerated the situation. The use of confrontation, whether individually or as a group, was never mentioned by Co-op Cab members.

Women and men at Co-op Cab attributed their anticipated grievance resolution strategies—formal and informal, respectively—partly to their company's identity as a worker co-operative. Women said that the formal empowerment derived from co-operative ideology and shared ownership enabled them to raise formal grievances. Men at the co-operative felt that these same elements allowed them greater access to worker-supervisors, thereby permitting them a choice of informal or formal means to resolve their disputes.

The legal consciousness at Co-op Cab was not unintentional. The co-operative made deliberate efforts to educate members about their rights and to empower them to raise grievances. Co-op Cab created a culture where members knew how to use the grievance system and were encouraged to resolve their disputes. Private Taxi, in contrast, had little concern for procedure and rights. Its grievance culture emphasized being "tough enough" not to need to bring a formal grievance and to be able to resolve disputes oneself. Thus, merely having certain structures in place – such as formal grievance procedures – does not guarantee a certain level of legal consciousness. The specific cultures of the individual institutions, such as the grievance cultures at Co-op Cab and Private Taxi, had a great impact on workers' legal consciousness.

Works Cited

Galanter, M. (1974). Why the 'Haves' Come Out Ahead: Speculations on the Limits of Legal Change. *Law & Society Review* 9:95–127.

Gusfield, J. (1967). Moral Passage: The Symbolic Process in Public Designations of Deviance. *Social Problems* 15:175–188.

Hoffmann, E.A. (2004). Selective Sexual Harassment: How the Labeling of Token Workers Can Produce Different Workplace Environments for Similar Groups of Women. *Law and Human Behavior* 28:29–45.

Hoffmann, E. (2005). Dispute Resolution in a Worker Co-operative: Formal Procedures and Procedural Justice. *Law & Society Review* 39:51–82.

6

Loyalty Instead of Leaving: Dispute Resolution in the Organics Industry[1]

Organic food distribution, as discussed in Chapter 3, is an industry that attracts some workers who are ideologically committed to organic foods or ethical business practices and others who might never have considered the moral, health, or ecological dimensions of food until they found jobs in the industry. Within the organics industry, I compared two British organic food distributors with similar missions and workforce demographics, one co-op and one conventional business. In the course of the study, I found distinct differences in the amount and the character of loyalty among the workers as well as differences in dispute resolution strategies.

Work and organization studies suggest that workers who are more loyal will be more likely to discuss problems, bring grievances, and confront disputes. At first, this might seem surprising, since one might assume that loyal workers might be those with fewer problems in their organizations. However, all workers encounter problems at work at some point, so in many cases those who are loyal to their organizations are the ones who "fight and stay," raising issues and bringing grievances. Because these workers are committed, they are willing to see an organization through difficult times, instead of quitting as soon as problems arise (Dowding et al. 2000; Hirschman 1970; Saunders et al. 1992). However, there is one exception to this: if the workers' organizational commitment has a strong ideological component, these extremely committed workers might actually be more likely to quit if they feel their organization has betrayed their ideology (Hirschman 1970). In this case, the intensity of their

1   Small portions of this chapter have been previously published in Exit and Voice: Organizational Loyalty and Dispute Resolution Strategies. (2006). *Social Forces* 84:2313–2330.

commitment becomes the basis of their repulsion with the disloyal organization and propels them to leave.

Loyalty

Employees at the conventional whole food organization, HealthBite, often described their paychecks as motivation for their jobs. A few were motivated by attraction to the organics movement and took their jobs to pursue this ideological commitment (and for the employee discount on the more expensive organic food). However, most others simply saw their positions as easily accessible, low-skill jobs that provided a decent wage. Many had stumbled into their current jobs through word-of-mouth or by answering ads in the newspaper. In interviews, the employees spoke about loyalty infrequently; when they did express such sentiments, they spoke of loyalty to the goals of the industry as a whole. "I care about organic food, taking care of my body, and taking care of the environment," one woman told me. "With this job, I can help other people get more involved with organic food."

On the other hand, workers at Organix Co-op, more so than workers at any of the other co-ops in this study, were committed not only to their organization, but also to the ideals of worker co-operatives. Many members said they had intentionally sought out Organix because they wanted to be part of a co-operative work environment. Some had left more highly paid jobs in the private sector to take jobs, and others commuted well over an hour to work there. Many of these workers could talk at length about co-operative ideology, the history of the co-operative movement, and the main tensions between worker co-operative practice and theory. The worker co-operative members consistently made statements about their loyalty to the organization. For example, one of the workers at Organix Co-op described her commitment to the co-operative:

> You're part of a special organization. Sometimes it's about this special feeling because you're working individually, but you don't finish until everyone is finished. The work is always done at the end of the day. And, ideally, it is done as a team. You run around like mad and help everybody else … In a [conventional] workplace, you're expected to just do your own job and go home. No one cares.

These contrasts resulted in substantial differences in dispute resolution strategies at these two organics companies. Employees at HealthBite rarely addressed their workplace problems at all. Instead, they created various coping strategies and left the jobs if their workplace became intolerable. Workers at Organix Co-op resolved disputes both informally and through formal means, and rarely spoke about toleration; however, they were willing to quit if they felt the co-operative no longer acted according to certain ideological principles.

Dispute Resolution at HealthBite

The employees at HealthBite relied nearly exclusively on informal routes to resolve problems, with no one mentioning the formal dispute mechanisms that were available at the company: "We've got a complaint procedure we go to if we've got a complaint," one worker told me. "They try and solve it. But really we're on our own."

When HealthBite employees did attempt to resolve workplace problems, they were more likely to rely on informal methods. For example, this woman who had worked at HealthBite for two years as a stockroom worker, said:

> *Even though I might be right, if we end up sorting it out—even legally—I've still got to work here at the end of the day. And it's just so much easier if you can sort it out between yourselves. So [what if] you get an official piece of paper saying, "They're wrong, I'm right?"*

One woman contrasted her experiences at HealthBite with her previous civil service job: "I guess it's all handled much more on an individual basis. If someone bothers you, you are to call on the guy and say 'Don't do that; don't speak to me like that.'"

One of the men, who worked as a packer, explained that informal dispute resolution could sometimes turn into arguments. But he did not characterize this behavior as malevolent:

> *We all argue with one another [laughs]. There's nothing personal. Or we just say, "Right we've got to sort that out today" and just voice our opinions. Normally, it gets sorted out one way or another.*

However, some people did not believe they were capable of engaging in informal dispute resolution. Below, one senior woman explained how she sometimes engaged in informal dispute resolution on behalf of other workers:

> *I'm the strong character, so I pretty much stand up for myself. There've been occasions when there've been [others who] felt that there've been injustices and they've come to me. And I've sort of pushed on their behalf because I've worked more closely with [the two owners] and maybe I know them better than some of the other staff. And maybe the staff feel they can't approach the directors or they're not sure how they'll take something. So I'll quite happily go in there with them or go in there on their behalf and say, "So-and-so is not happy with this."*

Since many HealthBite workers felt unable to raise issues, they would often develop ways of coping with their problems at work (toleration) or they would choose to leave.

TOLERATION

HealthBite workers mentioned toleration strategies more frequently than members of Organix Co-op. In the representative quote below, a HealthBite employee explained that often his preferred path is to do nothing:

> *If someone else isn't doing their work and I'm doing it all, what I've learned in the past is to just shut your mouth and keep doing it. 'Cause that's how it works. I just shut up and keep doing it.*

These employees had developed various ways to cope with problems they could not—or would not—resolve. Their ability to tolerate allowed them to avoid any sort of dispute resolution, formal or informal, and yet remain in their jobs. A number of employees at the company emphasized their abilities to push past problems and accomplish their work; this helped them avoid leaving their jobs.

EXIT

Approximately one-sixth of the employees I interviewed at HealthBite mentioned exiting as a strategy for dealing with problems. These workers felt that quitting was an easy option if they found themselves unhappy at their jobs. For example, a woman who had worked at HealthBite for a little more than a year said the following:

> *What I'm getting here, I know I could get in another job. I can go to an agency and get another job. So I'm not fighting for a career here. It's just a casual job and I'm not going to fight to keep it. If there was something I really couldn't stand, then I would move on.*

HealthBite employees reasoned that their jobs are easily replaced and, therefore, quite disposable. Quitting would lead to the minor inconvenience of finding a new position, but it would help them avoid the hassle of confrontation or learning to cope with unresolved problems.

Dispute Resolution at Organix Co-operative

Members of Organix Co-op frequently preferred formal grievance resolution to informal measures. For example, one woman described a recent formal grievance that she later described as a simple dispute that probably could have been resolved informally, but the parties involved chose formal procedures instead. One woman said using the formal procedure helped keep small problems from "turn[ing] nasty" and escalating further.

Another worker echoed this belief:

> It's good that there's that [formal grievance] mechanism, because we're a big organization. Lots of people. Lots of personalities. Lots of different ideas about the way we should be going, and we've got to have some kind of formal, mutual way of sorting out problems if they get out of hand.

Similarly, this man described an instance when he felt frustrated with some aspects of the organization:

> It was just that the department wasn't acting in the way I wanted it to work. My relationship with the department was suffering and I thought that I couldn't get on with my job, so I took the whole of the department to grievance. It turned out that there was something available to me in terms of information or the way my job could be done to work better. So we worked it out quite well. I [had been] frustrated; I [had] thought about just leaving. Find something else. But I stayed and I saw it out. That wasn't the easy path, but stayed because I care. This isn't just a job.

Rather than quitting, he raised a formal grievance against his entire department. Although this was not easy for him to do, he felt he had a duty to put forth the effort of a formal grievance.

Members of Organix worker co-operative were more likely to mention informal dispute resolution among their strategies than their counterparts at HealthBite. For example, this woman, who had worked at Organix for more than a decade, explained how she would try resolving disputes informally first:

> I always try to address things informally first. Have a talk with someone. Tell them what's going on for you. Of course, sometimes they're not friendly about it, but you have to try to work things out. It's easier, if it works. If not, then you can always go to a [formal] grievance.

As the quotation above implies, the informal route sometimes provided an efficient method for resolving disputes. However, informal dispute resolution can also be a more subtle use of power in that it often circumvents much of the public debate that is inevitable with formal grievances. This man reflected on such power dynamics:

> I actually find that these formal procedures that we go through are much less divisive than the informal ones. The informal ones tend to arrive at a kind of consensus that nobody fully understands. And certainly, if you're affected by that decision, you may well feel that the decision is being taken in a way that isn't transparent. There are no committee meetings: they're informal, you know, passing through the corridor, and having a word, and saying, "What do you think about so-and-so?" They happen to be in groups of, maybe, two. Then those two go and meet another two, and so on. So they're not transparent, and I find that rather bad and undermining of the [co-operative] principles.

This worker also noted that the informal actions and negotiations involved might be less democratic.

People at Organix said they felt free to express anger openly, perhaps the most direct way to address problems informally. The following woman worked on the payroll and collected orders. She gave the following example of how she felt free to lose her temper:

> I used to do the wages on a Monday, and I wanted to change it to a Friday. I talked to the appropriate people and thought it was all agreed and set up. Then it came to the moment of the change and this coincided with the start of a new training year for me, so it was essential that things were worked out, because, by then, I needed to do the wages on a

Friday. But once that time came, the most crucial person, the one doing the scheduling, said, "What's all this about?" as though he'd never heard any of it. I was absolutely furious. We had a big row.

At Organix, this woman had the freedom to show her rage. She was not afraid that she would lose her job or pay dearly in some other way. Later, she said that she had apologized for yelling, but still maintained that if such a stressful situation happened again, she might not be able to contain herself.

TOLERATION

Less than a third of the workers at Organix spoke of developing the ability to tolerate problems, rather than resolve them. Those workers who did were often disempowered due to race or class. For example, a Sikh worker felt that neither formal nor informal dispute resolution were successful options for him. He described an incident where a co-worker offended him by deliberately flipping off his head covering. When he brought a grievance, he was not satisfied with the outcome. He just learned, as he said, to "grit my teeth and just get on with life." He explained that he is able to tolerate racist and other offensive behavior because he is strong as an individual. If he could not get satisfaction when he asserted himself, he was strong enough to be able to tolerate the circumstances.

Another Organix worker described her reluctance to address grievances, either formally or informally.

No place is perfect; nobody's perfect. You can't let things bother you. I mean, this place isn't perfect, and sometimes it makes me quite mad, but you can't get worked up about things. I find, if I just step back, whatever is a problem one day, doesn't bother me so much the next day. If you raise it as a grievance – or even confront someone [about the problem] – then you're making it into a bigger deal. Just deal with it; step back; don't let things bother you so much.

This worker learned to tolerate problems and, thus, avoided any dispute resolution, formal or informal.

EXIT

About a quarter of Organix Co-op members mentioned quitting. This percentage is actually greater than that of HealthBite. At first glance, this might seem contrary to the predictions of earlier research on organizations and workplace disputes. It also appears to contradict the claims of worker co-op advocates who believe members of worker co-operatives have more avenues for resolving disputes successfully and, therefore, have little need to exit.

However, closer examination shows that Organix members did not feel the need to leave to resolve workplace disputes; their commitment to the co-operative was too great to allow them to simply opt out because of uncomfortable situations. Instead, they said that they would leave if the co-op abandoned its co-operative principles: "I think the only time I would leave is if Organix weren't Organix anymore," a young woman told me. "If it changed, no longer stood up for its goals, then why stay?"

Similarly, this man, who had been with Organix since shortly after it began, said he would leave if he felt the co-operative had betrayed its ideological goals:

> I'm here because it's a co-op. I'm here because the world needs more of this type of organization. It's a job that really syncs with my beliefs. If that changed, then I don't know what I'd do. I guess I'd leave.

Working at Organix meant more to its members than a paycheck, so the decision to exit would have to be over a substantial issue. This stood in stark contrast to HealthBite, where exiting to escape workplace problems was one of the main strategies employees discussed.

Conclusions

This chapter has explored a conventional business and a worker co-operative in the organic food industry. As in the other industries already discussed, the members of the co-operative were more able to address disputes through more mechanisms—formal and informal—than their counterparts in the conventional business. Workers who could not or would not raise their disputes either formally or informally—and who wished to remain at the organization—were left in the position of having to tolerate problems. Although toleration is not a strategy to actually resolve disputes, it was a way that some workers dealt with their workplace problems (Hoffmann 2006).

Interestingly, in this industry, Organix members were more likely than HealthBite workers to say they would quit their jobs to resolve a workplace problem. But upon closer examination, the reasons the workers considered leaving were different.

Workers at HealthBite felt their jobs were replaceable and disposable and that it would be easier in some cases to leave the company rather than get tangled up in resolving a dispute. In contrast, workers at Organix Co-op explained that they would quit only if they felt betrayed by the co-operative. The worker co-operative members' greater ideological commitment made them, ironically, more loyal, but also more likely to become frustrated and consider leaving (Hirschman 1970; Rothschild and Whitt 1986). Thus, their reasons for exit fit well into what some social scientists predict. For example, Hirschman asserts that "those [workers] who care the *most* about the quality of the product and who, therefore, are those who would be the most active, reliable, and creative agents of voice are, for that very reason, also those who are apparently likely to exit first in cases of deterioration [emphasis in original]"(Hirschman 1970: 47). With this in mind, it is not surprising that Organix Co-op, the co-op with the greatest ideological zeal, is also the organization whose members reported more exit strategies. Organix members said they would consider quitting if the co-operative adopted "wrongful" policies or made poor decisions that compromised the co-operative's integrity: this action would not serve as a way to resolve disputes; it would be a form of protest to register their disgust.

Works Cited

Dowding, K., John, P. Mergoupis, T. and Van Vugt, M. (2000). Exit, Voice and loyalty: Analytic and Empirical Developments. *European Journal of Political Research* 37:469–495.

Hirschman, A.O. (1970). *Exit, Voice, and Loyalty: Responses to Declines in Firms, Organizations, and States*. Cambridge: Harvard University Press.

Hoffmann, E.A. (2006). Exit and Voice: Organizational Loyalty and Dispute Resolution Strategies. *Social Forces* 84:2313–2330.

Rothschild, J. and Whitt, J.A. (1986). *The Co-operative Workplace: Potentials and Dilemmas of Organizational Democracy and Participation*. Cambridge: Cambridge University Press.

Saunders, D.M., Sheppard, B.H., Knight, V. and Roth, J. (1992). Employee Voice to Supervisors. *Employee Responsibilities & Rights Journal* 5:241–259.

7

Co-operative Struggles: Struggles Toward the Goal of Equality[1]

As businesses owned and managed by their workers, worker co-operatives strive for inclusiveness and equality. Often formed by ideologically committed activists, these businesses often seek to not only share the profits among their workers, but also create workplaces with heightened workplace justice. Indeed, many of the co-operatives' members hoped that an aspect of belonging to a worker co-operative was not only greater worker power, but heightened equality among the workers. Nevertheless, differences among the workers in education, class, and gender can complicate application of the co-operatives' egalitarian ideals. Such challenges are not unexpected. Indeed, co-operative observers often assert that "[o]nce a co-operative increases in size, complexity and, above all, worker-heterogeneity, democratic decision-making simply becomes too cumbersome and conflictual" (Wright 2010: 168).

Two of the co-operatives studied in the research particularly struggled to create democratic workplaces, with equality among their many members: Co-op Cab and Organix Co-operative. At each co-operative, one group of workers enjoyed an "insider" status (Tyler and Lind 2000). At Co-op Cab, men were the insiders. At Organix Co-op, middle-class white workers were the insiders.

One of the biggest advantages of this insider status was that these workers could choose whether they wished to resolve their grievances formally or informally. In contrast, the other workers were able to bring formal grievances, but rarely could resolve issues informally.

---

1   Portions of this chapter have been previously published in Dispute Resolution in a Worker Co-operative: Formal Procedures and Procedural Justice. (2005). *Law & Society Review* 39:51–82 and in Selective Sexual Harassment: Differential Treatment of Similar Groups of Women Workers, (2004). *Law and Human Behavior* 28:29–45.

Co-op Cab

Although workers at Co-op Cab generally discussed two ways they anticipated resolving workplace grievances—(1) formally through the grievance resolution procedures provided by the organization, and (2) informally through negotiation and discussion with managers or co-workers—in actual practice, only the formal route was available to the women. Although nearly all the workers interviewed expressed appreciation for the formal grievance procedures, men and women differed with respect to anticipated dispute resolution strategy. Notably, the women at Co-op Cab were more likely than their male co-workers to raise formal grievances. When explaining why they felt able to bring grievances, women cited the ideology of equality and non-hierarchy, including the co-operative's structure and the Workers' Council, with its promise of formal procedural justice. Men also referred to the co-operative's ideology when explaining their anticipated grievance strategies, but, in contrast, their strategies rarely involved formal procedures. The men at Co-op Cab anticipated settling grievances informally, perceiving the formal grievance process as only a last resort. They cited the co-operative's ideology of equality and non-hierarchy to assert that the more egalitarian relationships between workers and worker-managers permitted greater availability of informal resolution options. Unlike their female co-workers, the men at Co-op Cab did not express a need to rely on formal processes to feel assured of procedural justice: they perceived just treatment in formal or informal settings. While both men and women did anticipate times when they would not raise formal grievances, the men, in situations in which they would not raise formal grievance, still had the option of informal resolution, while women could only decide whether to act formally or not act at all. Additionally, a few individuals had doubts about the Council. Although these members included both men and women, men used their misgivings to justify not using the formal grievance system; yet women, despite their doubts, still anticipated using the formal grievance system, their only option.

FORMAL GRIEVANCE RESOLUTION

While both men and women at Co-op Cab voiced appreciation for the grievance procedures, women more frequently anticipated bringing formal grievances. All interviewed women emphasized that the Workers' Council provides an avenue for redress that is rarely available at other businesses, stressing that their membership in the co-operative gave them the right to use the Council. The statement by the woman below illustrates this attitude; she said that the formal dispute resolution process does not intimidate workers since the co-op encourages members to use the Workers' Council, a feature that is rarely found in conventional organizations. A year before the time of the interview, this driver had accumulated too many accident points, so management subsequently removed her from driving shifts, allowing her only to work in the office. She appealed the decision and lost. Nevertheless, her statement expresses the attitude that the best way to have a problem addressed is through a formal grievance:

> *People aren't afraid to bring grievances if they feel they've got one.*
> *We're encouraged to use the Workers' Council if we feel that we have a*
> *grievance ... I think there's a sort of a sense that there's very few jobs*
> *where you have that opportunity, so make the most of it.*

Another woman's experience with the Workers' Council came from serving as a member of the Council, rather than raising a grievance. This woman expressed her intention to use the Workers' Council even though she realized that pursuing an appeal could be arduous and emotionally taxing. Like her female co-workers, she, too, trusted that she would receive procedural justice from the Workers' Council:

> *People are really glad [the Workers' Council is] there because as hard as*
> *it may be to actually go through the process, it's easy to go through the*
> *process. It's just more of an emotional thing: what's going to happen?*
> *I wouldn't hesitate to appeal because I know that's what the Workers'*
> *Council is there for, to hear what I have to say.*

These women articulated their anticipated strategy of using the company's formal grievance procedures, trusting that the formal grievance procedures would deliver procedural justice.

In explaining their grievance strategies, many women described instances when they or another woman experienced informal injustice, but successfully secured formal justice through the grievance procedures. For example, another woman recalled a situation in which a woman who had been unjustly fired successfully appealed to the Workers' Council:

> *Management tried to get rid of a woman who was working in our office.*
> *They fired her not just from her office position but from the co-op as*
> *a whole. I felt that they hadn't treated her right. She came to me and*

asked me to represent her even though I wasn't a [an official co-worker advocate volunteer].

I felt that management had really screwed up. They fired her based on an evaluation that was arbitrary—there hadn't been a regular evaluation. Suddenly, they develop all sorts of problems with her work and suddenly they canned her. I felt that what was really at issue was that she had said something rude. There were problems with her work, but I think also the person that made the decision was under a lot of stress at the time. I think that he lost it, he exploded at her.

It went to a Workers' Council. They both had to sit down together and hear each other's side. He didn't want to. He was still upset. But so was she. And, in the end, she won.

Her recollection of how the Workers' Council treated this fired woman strengthened this woman's confidence in the formal grievance process's ability to guarantee justice.

Relating her own experiences, a long-time night driver described a confrontation she had with a female member of the board of directors who tried to have her fired. She appealed to the Workers' Council who entirely removed the discipline letter from her file:

I was scared because this person is currently on the board and what was said when it happened was, "That's it. That's your job. That's a twelve point letter," meaning, "I'm going to go after your job, bitch, I'm going to have you fired." So it was scary, but I was satisfied. We both went before the Workers' Council. I think she had someone with her, and I brought [a co-worker advocate]. In the end, they heard my side.

Her own experiences with the formal grievance procedures furthered her belief that the Workers' Council makes justice possible.

However, the men rarely anticipated using the formal grievance procedures. For example, one man described a time when a male supervisor marked him as tardy, which generated a discipline letter that deducted money from his paycheck. Although he initially cited this situation as something he would "unquestionably" raise as a formal grievance, in fact, he had not appealed the tardiness issue with the Council: rather, he raised the issue informally with his worker-manager who removed the formal discipline letter from his file, without any grievance hearing, formal investigation, or official recognition that he had or had not been unjustly penalized. He achieved justice without engaging the formal mechanisms:

> *Could you give me an example of something that you would unquestionably take to the Council?*
>
> *I was marked down as being tardy, and [I] investigated it, and found out that I wasn't tardy, so I brought it to the worker-manager's attention. I was able to document what was correct or wasn't correct about the discipline. It takes a significant amount of time and energy to appeal something on a Workers' Council, so you just make the decision whether or not you're interested in making a stink about something or not. But, I always feel empowered to. I always feel like I have that option.*

Thus, even though this man felt he had the option of a formal grievance, he still perceived the process negatively. Although he considered the Workers' Council an important option to have available, he characterized it negatively as "making a stink" that would require a great deal of time and energy.

INFORMAL GRIEVANCES

Unlike their female co-workers, men expressed a greater likelihood to resolve grievances informally, only anticipating raising a formal grievance when blatant, intentional mistreatment occurred. Ninety percent of the men at Co-op Cab interviewed stated that a benefit of working at a co-operative was the ease of informal grievance resolution. These men felt that the co-operative's informality permitted problems between co-workers and managers, or among co-workers, to be addressed more easily without raising formal grievances.

The man below, for example, explained that being part of a co-op was being part of a team: that team mentality reassured him that formal grievances were not necessary, and, perhaps, not even appropriate. He believed that he would be more likely to raise a formal grievance at a conventional business because, there, the workplace atmosphere encouraged workers to look out for themselves. In contrast, he felt more encouraged to work as part of a team for the collective goals at a worker co-operative:

At Co-op Cab I'm not working for someone with control over me. I'm part of a team with other people. We all help each other and work together. [In contrast], [previous job] is always trying to squeeze every ounce of work out of you. So, I think I'd be more likely to bring a grievance somewhere else.

In addition, this man said that he would be more likely to bring a formal grievance in a conventional business because that would be the only way to have his concerns addressed. He said he would be less likely to bring a grievance at the co-operative since there he had more informal avenues to resolve any problems:

I think I'd be more likely to bring a grievance somewhere else, because there would be no other way to get to them, to get to the manager. Here, you know, I can just go talk to [the operations manager] after work or whatever, and just say, "Hey ..." Like, whatever. And just talk to him.

However, this type of grievance resolution is only possible for workers who are within informal networks with those workers who possess greater power at Co-op Cab: the worker-managers and, to some extent, the dispatchers, who supervise shifts and administer discipline. Informal resolution of grievances can be casually raised with a manager or a dispatcher only when the concerned party is socially situated so that informal negotiation can occur. This socializing during off-time, or informally during work-time, often includes the discussion and resolution of problems: informal dispute resolution.

At Co-op Cab, only men were part of the networks with managers and dispatchers that facilitated informal dispute resolution. The impact of camaraderie among male workers on dispute resolution strategies was particularly intense because worker-managers and supervisor-dispatchers were all, with one exception, men. Workers at Co-op Cab often socialized with other workers in off-hours. However, because much of this socializing was sex segregated, male workers had greater contact and familiarity with the worker-managers and dispatchers, resulting in friendships and informal networks. The following comment by a man who mostly drove the rush-hour (late afternoon) shift, illustrates the level of familiarity between male managers and male workers expressed by all but two of the men interviewed:

Some people don't like Gary [the personnel manager]. Like Helen, I know she hates him, but I think he's great. He's really funny. Actually,

*I play cards with him and some other guys every other Tuesday. He's
a great guy.*

In describing his regular socializing with and fondness for the personnel
manager, Tom also stated that a female co-worker did not share his feelings.

Unlike this man, above, the woman quoted below did not socialize with
the managers and dispatchers. She believed that the greater familiarity and
closeness among men resulted in preferential treatment by the worker-
managers:

> *It's like a male bonding club. Like, "These are extenuating circumstances
> for you. I think I can help you out here." I do believe that the upholding
> of procedures applies to women more than it does to men. The worker-
> managers do their best to uphold the maximum point system when
> women are involved, and tend to be more lax about these procedures
> when men are involved. The worker-managers, I call them "typical
> males." [laughs/sighs] And they have this sort of bonding club with
> other men in general. And might not even realize what they're doing.
> But maybe feeling that, "Well, this is a woman, she'll put up with it."
> Or whatever. Not necessarily feeling the incentive to give this person
> [woman] a break.*

The juxtaposition of these two quotes underscores how the men experienced
greater "trust" in the co-operative's informal workings. Even in very informal
situations, the men perceived what Tyler and Lind referred to as a "level playing
field" (Tyler and Lind 2000: 76). In contrast, women perceived discriminatory
treatment from managers, lacking "trust" and faith in "neutrality" with regard
to both specific individual managers and the informal workings of the co-
operative generally (Tyler and Lind 2000).

Like the other women interviewed, the woman quoted below also believed
that the greater familiarity between male workers and male managers not only
gave men an edge with the managers, but also placed women workers at a
distinct disadvantage:

> *I really think that a lot of men at the co-op try to be inclusive of women
> or not openly discriminatory, but whether they choose to admit it to
> themselves or not, they are often more comfortable with men. In fact,
> I do think that's also why I was put back on probation when I came*

> *back. [Worker-manager] went according to policy and put me back on*
> *probation. Since I was a woman and we weren't really buddy-buddy, he*
> *wouldn't have felt really comfortable <u>not</u> going according to procedure.*
> *And I think that's why a lot of decisions at the co-op are made the way*
> *they are.*

This camaraderie between male managers and male workers also affected men's anticipation of using only informal grievance resolution. The men reported a greater casualness around resolving grievances and emphasized that the possibility of such informal dispute resolution represented one of the benefits of Co-op Cab. Another male cab driver explained his belief that, because he can interact with the managers very informally, the formal grievance procedure is never necessary:

> *There's a whole grievance procedure, yeah, but it's like, you're part of a*
> *family. You can just talk to the other people. It's not like the manager is*
> *your "boss." There isn't any one boss. You can just go talk to him. You*
> *can even curse him out if you want to, and he can't really do anything*
> *to you. Of course, he won't be pleased. [laughs]. But I can't imagine*
> *bringing him to the [formal grievance procedures of the] Workers'*
> *Council. I couldn't do that.*

Similarly, this driver's analogy to inclusion in a family also underlines a theme that some men mentioned: that their "insider" status both permitted them the option of informal grievance resolution, but also somewhat discouraged them from using the formal grievance procedures. On an informal level, the men at Co-op Cab were confident of the trust, neutrality, and standing they had and so felt assured that they could informally receive justice. An aspect of this inclusion, however, was that they were inhibited from bringing formal grievances. As insiders, the men interpreted use of the formal procedures as demonstrating that they, themselves, failed or that the co-operative failed to work properly. Only when, and if, they were no longer included among the insiders who could rely on informal justice, would they move out of "group mode" and need to use the formal procedures to receive procedural justice.

The quotes above illustrate men's greater "standing" in the co-operative in informal settings, with easy unofficial access to the (male) managers and dispatchers. While both men and women members were proud of their formal membership in the co-operative, the women did not experience the informal inclusiveness, such as the feeling of being "a family." Importantly, although both men and women were members of the co-operative, only men had the informal "standing" to participate in the social networks with other men, including the managers and dispatchers.

By perceiving procedural justice at the informal as well as formal level, the men at Co-op Cab moved into what Tyler and Lind (2000) call "group mode." They expected fair treatment and, therefore, acted co-operatively. Part of this co-operative "group mode" ethic was that the men considered formal grievance resolution to be inappropriate, although possibly a procedurally just and effective option. While the women at Co-op Cab did not seem to enter "group mode" strongly (not necessarily expecting fair treatment or feeling pressure to avoid the formal grievance procedures), neither did they enter "individual mode" (Tyler and Lind 2000), in that their focuses were not exclusively on their own immediate gains. Instead, women maintained a quest for justice and other more philosophical rather than material immediate goals.

TOLERATION

Although men's and women's perceptions of formal and informal grievance resolution differed, both men and women anticipated times when they would not raise formal grievances. However, men, in situations in which they would not raise formal grievance, still had the option of informal resolution, while women could only decide whether to act formally or not act at all. For example, another woman who began driving cab as an undergraduate stated that she preferred to "wait out" certain negative situations rather than using her time and energy to fight:

> It's like, how much am I willing to put up with? How much energy do I feel like putting into paperwork and filing a grievance and trying to articulate relatively minor things to other people? Not necessarily that they are really minor, but I don't have that energy. It's like, is it easier to fight for certain things or is it easier to put up with it and wait through it 'til you get to the end of it?

Like the other women, she believed that her options were either to raise a formal grievance or to do nothing. Thus, learning to tolerate the situation, "lumping it" (Galanter 1974), was women's primary alternative to using the formal grievance system.

In contrast, men were unlikely to mention toleration (only one man mentioned this). For them, the question was one of choosing among alternative methods rather than between action or inaction. That is, they chose between ways of addressing grievances—formal or informal resolution—not between whether or not to address the grievance at all. The men emphasized their ability to talk with the supervisors. They believed that interpersonal skills sufficed to resolve conflict, as this man explains below:

> You can't get so worked up. Like some people get all worked up and bring a grievance about everything. That's their right; that's ok. But, me, I like to just talk to the person. Like if I think a dispatcher isn't treating me fairly, I'll just go and talk to the guy and reason with him. I don't get all excited.

In anticipating not using the formal grievance procedures, this driver isn't forced to "lump it," but can choose an informal strategy. This option, however, is only available to those workers who can "just go and talk to the guy" supervisor—an option not available to the women workers at Co-op Cab.

APPREHENSIONS ABOUT FORMAL PROCEDURES

Finally, while most members, men and women alike, expressed their appreciation for and confidence in the Workers' Council, a few individuals had misgivings about the Council. Although these members included both men and women, men used their doubts to justify not using the formal grievance system; yet women, despite their doubts, still anticipated using the formal grievance system. The women explained that it was their only option.

The two men interviewed who expressed doubts about the Workers' Council cited these doubts as their motivation to try to resolve problems informally. They believed that they would be more successful if they tried to confront the manager personally. One of these men said:

> The burden of proof has slipped from being on management to being on the appellant. It didn't used to be that way. There's a lot less appealing of discipline things [now]. More people are just going, "Well, I'm gonna lose anyway. So I'm just gonna take the letter, and I'll go in and schmooz and lie and cry and throw myself on the mercy of management to get a lesser disciplinary letter."

In this way, he used his critique of the Workers' Council to justify his future strategy of informal grievance resolution.

However, two women at Co-op Cab had similar concerns about the effectiveness of appealing to the Workers' Council, but did not use these doubts to justify abandoning the strategy of formal grievances. Instead, they anticipated bringing grievances *despite* their apprehensions about the fairness of the process and the low likelihood of advantageous decisions by the Council. Notwithstanding these concerns about the Workers' Council, they approached the formal grievance process as the correct—and only—option open to them. If the women did not bring their grievances to the Workers' Council, no other means of resolving their grievances existed.

One of these two women who expressed concern about the formal process describes, below, her doubt in the neutrality of the process and her lack of trust in the Captain of the Workers' Council. She believed that he was biased against her and might sway the decision against her:

> The captain of the Workers' Council doesn't get a vote in the Workers' Council, but he kind of helps mediate the whole thing. I mean, even though the mediator doesn't get a vote, just by the way they say things and the way they, you know, it's very hard to be an unbiased mediator. The guy who was a mediator, [name], at one point I told him I was appealing [her case]. He came by the office and basically tried to talk me out of appealing. He said that I didn't have a chance, that all the stuff wasn't valid, and started yelling at me in the parking lot. Literally yelling. And in the end I was, well, I said I didn't feel like I was going to get a fair hearing because he was obviously biased in one way. And even though he didn't get a vote, he wasn't, I didn't think, capable of keeping his opinions out of it. I think anybody who yells at somebody in a parking lot is going to say something during the Workers' Council to try to sway the Workers' Council, too. I'm still planning to appeal it, of course; that's why the Workers' Council is there.

Although this driver did not trust the authorities handling the dispute ("trust") and did not believe that she would receive non-discriminatory treatment ("neutrality"), she maintained confidence in her full status in the group ("standing"), at least in terms of her official status as a member with certain rights.

Similarly, another woman, who had joined the co-operative shortly after it formed and so was nearly a founding member, expressed doubts about neutrality and trust, but was also sufficiently confident in her official "standing" that she could demand to be heard. This driver had brought several grievances before the Workers' Council and anticipated bringing more in the future:

> I lost by one vote on the board decision. They ruled against me that I couldn't have my day before my Workers' Council, my peers. I filed another thing with them and I said, "I think you're mistaken and that's why I wrote this long letter. " I went before them again and said, "you're leaving me no alternative but to go outside of my co-operative, because my co-operative structure is not set up for me to be heard by my peers." [So then you decided you'd have to sue?] Yeah, that's basically what I meant. They had another vote and I lost by one vote again, so I hired an attorney. I sued them. It was a very rough year. There were things all over the bulletin board that anybody who sues their own co-operative should get the f*ck out if they're not happy. It's like, if you don't love your country, leave it, so to speak.

Some of her co-workers believed that if she had been a loyal member, she wouldn't have sued. However, she and others believed that the truly disloyal behavior would have been to exit without trying to resolve the problems at hand. In this way, if she had embraced "individual mode," she might have abandoned the co-operative and found employment elsewhere (a relatively easy option with the town's extremely low unemployment). Instead, she remained loyal to the co-operative by refusing to leave and, instead, fighting from within (see Hirschman 1970).

This same woman also discussed a more recent grievance she brought to the Workers' Council over discipline she considered preposterous, which bordered on harassment. Despite her absence of "trust" and her perception of no "neutrality," to this driver, failure to appeal to the Workers' Council would forfeit her rights as a co-operative member ("standing"). Her belief in her standing both permitted and forced her to try to receive justice through the formal grievance procedures:

> [After describing several decisions by worker-managers that she found blatantly unjust.] I have a temper. They were hoping I'd lose my temper and tell them to stick the place up their ass and quit. Each time I haven't done that. I've gone through their process no matter how much I knew that the odds were against me. Sometimes I win.

Thus, she maintained her faith in the formal grievance processes and her duty—as well as her entitlement—as a member to benefit from those processes. While she was not assured that she would triumph, she did believe the formal procedures provided the possibility of justice. She, like other women, maintained sufficient belief in their standing in the co-operative to conclude that they deserved to have their grievances heard, but they also were aware that their only avenue was the formal route, the grievance resolution procedures.

Organix Co-op

As at Co-op Cab, some members of Organix Co-op were more able to use both formal and informal routes than other members were. Rather than falling along gender lines, at Organic Co-op, members who felt less able to resolve grievances informally were members who were less formally educated, came from lower socio-economic status, and were non-white. However, these less-empowered members, like the women at Co-op Cab, were still very able to bring formal grievances.

Recall that Organix Co-op's previous location had been in a college town and employed many graduates from the large university there. When its commercial success meant that it needed a larger building, Organix Co-op moved to a formerly industrial, now economically depressed working-class town. At its previous location, Organix Co-op drew from the mostly white college students. In its new community, more working-class and non-white members joined with the middle-class members who moved with Organix Co-op to its new town.

FORMAL GRIEVANCE RESOLUTION

Despite some members' inability to address problems informally, these workers felt that having a realistic and useable formal grievance system was, in itself, very powerful. Many members explained that a key advantage of a worker co-operative was that formal grievances were more socially acceptable and easier to raise. For example, a woman from Organix who had been at the co-operative for five years, but was considering leaving to earn a college degree, emphasized the importance of having a formal grievance procedure:

> It's good that there's that [formal grievance] mechanism, because we're
> a big organization. Lots of people. Lots of personalities. Lots of different

> *ideas about the way we should be going, and we've got to have some*
> *kind of formal, mutual way of sorting out problems if they get out of*
> *hand.*

This woman had trust in the formal grievance resolution processes of the co-operative, and believed that these processes' sufficient neutrality would create a more equitable means of working out problems. She perceived everyone as having standing to bring formal grievances; this standing justifying embracing an "individual mode" (Tyler and Lind 2000).

Sometimes Organix Co-op members preferred resolving even apparently simple disputes formally. For example, one woman, who had worked full-time at the co-operative for six years since she was 17 years old, described a recent formal grievance at Organix:

> *[It's] just a difference of opinion in some cases. If somebody has just*
> *purely a difference of opinion on whatever it might be. That can*
> *sometimes turn nasty and can end up being taken to grievance.*
>
> *[Interviewer: When you say, "Turn nasty," what do you mean?]*
>
> *Well, just maybe each other's working practices are ... I can't think of*
> *an example ... Oh, one taken to grievance was over machinery, the way*
> *somebody operated machinery and the person didn't agree with [that*
> *person's] working practice.*

Similarly, another member who came from Organix's surrounding working-class community described a grievance that he had brought that others might have been able to resolve informally. "My relationship with the department was suffering and I thought that I couldn't get on with my job, so I took the whole of the department to grievance."

These workers felt the formal procedure was the right route for them. Yet, such disputes often could be resolved informally by "insider" members of the co-operative. However, without access to informal dispute mechanisms, formal grievance resolution and entering "individual mode" was necessary (Tyler and Lind 2000).

INFORMAL GRIEVANCE RESOLUTION

Others, in particular the white men at Organix, preferred resolving disputes through informal routes, as explained by this long-time member from Organix Co-op, who joined when he was a student at the local university:

> Some people like to bring formal grievances. But I like to get away from [the organization] and just sit down in the pub and have a chat.

These "insiders," who felt able to resolve disputes both informally and formally, often expressed a preference for the informal route, like the men at Co-op Cab.

A Japanese-British member of Organix asserted that successful informal grievance resolution was only an option for certain members:

> You either get listened to or you don't. It's not necessarily because of the job you have; it's the person you are usually. I find it's personalities more than anything else in this place that either stop people or help people..

> [Organix Co-op is] one of those situations where you feel like you should be equal but you are not necessarily equal because you don't necessarily have the same knowledge as somebody else or you haven't been here as long or you don't have the same sort of status.

Although this woman mentioned "personalities" as the key to power, she explained this by citing knowledge, tenure, and socio-economic status — attributes linked with being middle-class and white at Organix Co-op, not personality characteristics.

TOLERATION

Sometimes workers at Organix also preferred to take no action. For example, the following worker at Organix Co-op, described how his lack of formal education—leaving school at age 15—denied him the standing he felt was necessary to participate more in the running of the co-operative. He spoke of his strategy to "not put my head above the parapets." Here, he explained:

> You don't want to be the one who starts waving a finger. We all make mistakes and if you start talking about someone else's they may bring

up one or two of yours … As long as I'm doing what I can, I just forget it. So things that really ought to be put right, carry on. Just go on and on and on. [I don't want to be] the person who takes a person to grievance or disciplinary hearing.

This man had explained that when he felt some problem simply had to be addressed and could no longer be tolerated, he would ask someone with a middle-class accent to raise the grievance. He justified this strategy by asserting that this allowed those who "talked the right way" to raise important issues. He explained, "I'm not a wordsmith; I've had no university education and words don't come easily to me." This reluctance to try to resolve grievances either formally or informally meant that some workers had learned to tolerate problems.

APPREHENSIONS ABOUT FORMAL PROCEDURES

As at Co-op Cab, some workers at Organix Co-op also had some ambivalence about formal grievances. Members who were "insiders" and could resolve issues informally often used their criticism of the formal process as their reason for resolving disputes informally (similar to the men at Co-op Cab). Members who were not able to resolve issues informally (like the women at Co-op Cab) continued to anticipate using the formal processes despite criticisms similar to those raised by their "insider" co-workers. One example of a worker who had been disappointed with his recent formal grievance, yet anticipated still using the formal grievance procedures, was a Sikh worker. This member, who identified himself as Black, having been born in Pakistan and raised in a working-class northern England town, felt that neither formal nor informal grievance resolution were options for him. In the following quote, he explained how another worker had intentionally flipped off his head covering, greatly offending him. At that time, he did bring a formal grievance, but he felt that nothing was done.

From my sector, like Asia or Pakistan, I'm the only one who has lasted. Once an incident actually happened where I felt quite abused. I was wearing a cap, not my turban. I still believe [the co-worker] would know [that this cap counted as a head covering]. And [the co-worker] walked past and he just flipped my hat off and it fell on the floor. I was really, really fuming. People know who I am or that my beliefs are that way. I don't have to tell anybody. I brought [a grievance], but nothing actually happened.

I know there's a few [other non-white workers], but from my sector, like Asia or Pakistan, I'm the only one who has lasted—I've only lasted this long because I'm a fighter. I am an individual. [Some] people have other people backing them up and when I say something I don't have anybody backing me up. The only person backing me up is myself.

This worker was able to bring a formal grievance, but had been unsatisfied with how it was resolved; he lacked "trust" and doubted the "neutrality" of the grievance procedures. Nevertheless, he felt he had sufficient "standing" to be able to bring a grievance and felt that he could bring other formal grievances in the future (Tyler and Lind 2000). He expressed some doubt as to whether he would actually get satisfaction from future formal grievances, but he was willing and able to at least try.

Exclusion by Insiders

The insiders—men at Co-op Cab and middle-class whites at Organix Co-op— excluded their co-workers from the connections necessary to resolve their grievances informally in various ways. Although neither group of insiders was highly conscious of this exclusion, and might even have been shocked to be accused of it, the exclusion by the insiders was persistent.

ORGANIX CO-OP

At Organix Co-op, the exclusion of other members by the insiders was very subtle. At several meetings, insider members would throw about polysyllabic words that could easily be seen as unnecessarily long and used, it might seem, primarily to obfuscate the discussion, demonstrate their ability to use such long words, and underline that the speaker is a better-educated insider. Such techniques in emphasizing class differences also occurred informally. This could directly impact how grievances could be addressed. For example, one working-class white man who joined the co-op from the local community said:

I approached [the woman who made the work schedules] several times. The times she had given me just didn't work for me and my family's schedule. I tried to ask her about it, and she said she was too busy to talk to me. Then, I talked to [a middle-class member who had joined as a student at the university] and he encouraged me to talk to her again. Again, she wouldn't talk to me. I was going to [bring a formal grievance.] Then I sort of caught her as she was leaving and she had to talk with me. And she just kept saying that I didn't understand how things worked and how [the schedule] had to be. I went back to [the earlier mentioned middle-class member] and he went and talked to her, explained my family situation, and got everything sorted out. The thing is, at the end of the day, I know he didn't tell her anything different than what I had told her. But it was how he said it. He told her my family situation in a way that she was willing to hear, he used more important-sounding words and made my situation sound important enough for her to pay attention.

This exclusion by the scheduling woman was difficult for the speaker, above, to understand and overcome. She never was so blunt as to say that she wouldn't talk to him because he had a working-class accent or lacked a college degree. Indeed, if asked about this, she might have been horrified that her actions could be perceived as classist. Nevertheless, similar dynamics that resulted in some members being excluded from the access necessary to resolve concerns informally were found throughout Organix Co-op.

Similarly, racism was even more taboo so that an accusation of exclusion based on race would meet with even greater revulsion. Indeed, when workers at Organix Co-op did discuss exclusions based on race, often the speakers were quick to emphasize that race was not part of the dynamics, even though race seemed to play dominantly into the interactions discussed. For example, one Japanese-British woman made the comment that getting one's desired job rotations were easier to accomplish if one were white. When asked about this further, she said:

No, no. I mean, no. Its just that it seems that when [names several white men and women] have a problem with [the schedule] they always just get it sorted out easily. But when I or [mentions several non-white men and women] have a problem, we either have to just have the problem, or, like I was saying, if it gets really bad, I've [raised a formal grievance] over it.

Members of both groups of workers this woman mentioned were interviewed about formal and informal grievance resolution strategies. Indeed, the white workers whom she cited as being able to easily resolve scheduling difficulties informally spoke of being able to resolve a range of issues through informal resolution. The non-white workers whom she cited as having difficulty talked about the importance for formal grievance resolution for them at the co-operative.

CO-OP CAB

The exclusion of women at Co-op Cab involved a more complicated dynamic. At this cab company, men divided their women co-workers into two groups and assigned different labels to each group. Each group was excluded ·from access, but through two very different dynamics. The men categorized the women as either "lesbian" or "heterosexual." The label each woman received did not necessarily reflect the woman's self-identity, but rather reflected how her male co-workers perceived her and chose to treat her. Based on these labels, men sexually harassed some women, but actively avoided the others.

To be clear, the labels were distinct from women's own identities—sometimes the labels correlated with the woman's own self-identification, but other times they did not. Yet, in either situation, the labels had powerful effects on how the men treated their women co-workers and how these women experienced their workplace environment. However, the labels were not random or meaningless classifications. The labels "heterosexual" and "lesbian" implied certain types or stereotypes of women. Women whom the men labeled "heterosexual" were perceived by the men as inherently and always interested in romantic or sexual relationships with them. In contrast, the women whom the men labeled "lesbian" were seen as not only disinterested in intimate relations with the men co-workers, but as disdainful of all male contact.

All interviewed workers—self-labeled heterosexual, bisexual, and lesbian women and heterosexual men—described the company as having a workplace culture in which (heterosexual) men would treat different groups of women differently, based on which label a woman had—"lesbian" or "heterosexual." Men's statements support this assessment that their labeling was binary. Men often targeted women labeled "heterosexual," but rarely harassed women labeled "lesbian," as is discussed further below.[2]

---

2 Because a key aspect of this research involved people's perceptions of sexual harassment, I had the interviewees themselves define "sexual harassment." In many interviews, the term sexual harassment was brought up by the interviewees themselves. I deliberately chose not to offer a legal definition of harassment because I feared this official definition would inhibit the interviewees. Yet, regardless of whether or not the various behaviors described in this research all meet the precise legal definition of sexual harassment, these behaviors, nevertheless, caused the women experiencing them to avoid male co-workers and, therefore, to have fewer dispute resolution options.

For example, one female cab driver, who had been with the company for eight years, stated that if a woman was understood to be (that is, labeled) heterosexual, she would experience quite a bit of harassment:

> *I've hung out with a lot of people, men and women. Sometimes after work. I mean, if you're all hanging around at Co-op Cab, having a drink or just laughing, it's pretty much everyone. I think a lot of the lesbians don't get the type of harassment that heterosexual women do. The men don't see them as a pick-up line.*

Another woman, who mostly drove nights and who had been at the company for about seven years, preferred the men at the cab company to label her as a lesbian because she felt she was treated better by them when thus defined:

> *Sometimes I get treated like a lesbian, sometimes I get treated like a straight woman. I don't like being treated like a straight woman. I actually think there is [a difference in treatment]. Generally speaking, I prefer people think of me as a lesbian … I find people approach me with just a lot more ease if they perceive that I'm straight. The men have learned their lessons with the lesbians, to be a little more stand-offish. If they're single men, they treat the straight women like potential dates, someone to f*ck, and that is different.*

I was careful to triangulate my data on this phenomenon. "Triangulation" refers to collecting stories of the same phenomena from interviewees with very different perspectives. This allows the researcher to explore a given phenomenon—such as sexual harassment—from a variety of standpoints, thus, substantiating that the researcher's evolving understanding of the phenomenon is accurate and not simply reflecting the bias of an insular group of friends. By triangulating, I was able to confirm the dynamics the interviewees described, thus, heightening the validity of the data. To gather this information, I asked about men's accounts of themselves, men's accounts of other men's behavior, and women's accounts of men's behavior. Each way of gathering this data produced similarly accurate accounts.

The women at Co-op Cab were aware of which label the men had attached to the individual women. During the interviews, the women discussed what label they believed they and others had; they were well aware of whom the men perceived as heterosexuals or lesbians. I also spoke in-depth with some men about how they labeled and who had which label; the men, in their own interviews, confirmed the women's understandings of the labels' applications. Also, during these discussions, although usually at separate times during the interview, the men talked about how they interacted with various women co-workers. Thus, although I learned a great deal about the impact of labeling from the women, I confirmed this information with the men's reports. In the following sections, I do not provide each woman's assessments and the confirmation of these by her male co-workers. Since this would be lengthy and cumbersome without adding sufficiently to the discussion, I generally provide only the most illustrative quotations.

This "strategy" for avoiding sexual harassment by actively trying to be labeled lesbian is a strategy that several other women discussed. The experience reported by the woman quoted above and other women at Co-op Cab—that lesbian workers were harassed less and that the women often preferred a label of "lesbian" to "heterosexual"—is contrary to the findings of other researchers who document virulent harassment of lesbian workers at other businesses (e.g., Schneider 1982; Welsh 1999).

Some "testing" of this assertion about Co-op Cab's selective sexual harassment was provided by the experiences of two women whose labels changed. These data are particularly instructive, since they demonstrate that the labels had little to do with women's own identities and more to do with their male co-workers' perceptions and treatment of the women. The label of the first woman changed through her "coming out." The second woman's label changed when she openly began dating a man. They both reported that how they were treated changed when their labels changed.

The first woman had come out as a lesbian to only some of her co-workers at the time of the interview. She discussed how men's reactions to, and interactions with, her changed as she came out to more and more people at the cab company. Below, she describes an incident in which she stood up to a harasser who had labeled her "heterosexual." On this occasion, a male co-worker, in front of other drivers, asked her to meet him at the airport to have sex with him:

> I've had a couple of guys hit on me, harass me [make sexual, inappropriate inquiries] ... I can remember one of the guys was telling me, like, we're in the office in the afternoon. A bunch of us were getting ready to go and drive and this one guy had gotten the van, which is 59. You know, big deal, Cab 59. It's a van and we all know that. He was saying, "[Her name], why don't you meet me out at the airport, I got 59." "I'm like, what's up with that?" He says, "You know, it's so romantic, wouldn't it be fun if we could get in the back of the cab." And all this stuff. The other drivers kind of look at me and I said, "Dude, you'd better shut up now while you're ahead because you're coming close." You know? I kind of pointed my finger at him and told him, "You're really coming close to harassing me," and he said, "Well wouldn't you like it, blah-blah-blah?" and I'm like, "Stop, stop while you're ahead or there's gonna be a problem."

This first woman believed that sexual harassment had been an issue because she was not completely out to everyone at the cab company and was labeled by some men as heterosexual and by others as lesbian. She noted that all sexual harassment ended once everyone at the company understood her as lesbian.

The second woman related experiences in which she felt that sometimes men labeled her as heterosexual and treated her one way, and other times categorized her as lesbian and treated her another way. When labeled as heterosexual by the men, these co-workers interacted with her more regularly, although the interactions were not always pleasant. However, when she was labeled as lesbian, she had significantly less interaction with the men at work but avoided sexual harassment. For example, she observed different behaviors from male co-workers depending on the sex of her current partner—and, hence, the label ascribed to her:

> When I just started working here I was going out with a woman and then I started seeing a man ... If you're kind of established as a lesbian you don't get harassed by the men at work. Once it got out [that I then was dating a man], it's kind of open for question, some of them will try and make passes. I just don't like it. It's like if I was looking, believe me you'd know. It's not like you have to find it out.

This second woman concluded that when she first joined Co-op Cab she received much less harassment and less attention from men at the cab company because they labeled her as lesbian. Her experience is particularly illustrative when juxtaposed with the comments stating that new women employees receive especially trenchant sexual harassment, such as the woman quoted below:

> When I first started working at Co-op Cab, I'll tell you, I kind of felt like meat on the hoof. We had a lot of women working for us[3] but still it's a very much male-dominated profession and women put up with a lot of shit on the job and off ... So I had these guys really pressing on me hard ... These guys are dogging us constantly. I see it happen every time a new woman comes to work at the cab company.

Consistently, the women who reported sexual harassment as an ongoing problem had been labeled as heterosexual. This was true, regardless of whether these women self-identified as heterosexual, bisexual, or lesbian. As the woman

---

3   Actually, women at Co-op Cab comprise 16.3 percent of the workers at the cab company.

quoted above, the women at Co-op Cab viewed this behavior as an ongoing dynamic of the company culture.

The effect of sexual harassment was not always initially obvious to the women experiencing it. Although they acknowledged it immediately as unpleasant, sometimes they only later realized how their reaction to this harassment affected their own behavior. For example, one female driver who was labeled heterosexual described her experience when she initially tried to train for a dispatcher position which would have been a promotion, one of the positions in the cab company with more responsibility and status, and the perk of staying indoors on cold, icy Midwestern winter weeks. She recounted being driven out of the dispatch office, forfeiting her opportunity to gain the necessary training:

> *If you go and sit in the [dispatch] office when it's slow, that's called "slumming". So I kind of got in this habit. There would be other people slumming in there and people would be sitting around joking because it was pretty slow; dispatcher's not stressed out.*
>
> *I started to notice that these three guys in particular in the office sort of had these inside jokes going on while I was there. It took me a while to figure out that they decided that I was hanging out there because I had a crush on the dispatcher. When I got there, [one day] one of the other guys who was in there said, "Jake's not here today, he's in New York." Jake was the dispatcher. I don't remember what I said to them, but I remember I was pissed. I said something real nasty to him though, and he said, "Well just tell me. Don't you like Jake?" I said, "Yeah, I think Jake's a great guy. I think he's really smart and I think he's really witty. How come you don't think Frank has a thing for Jake. Frank is in the office all the time." And he said "Frank who? The only Frank I know is a guy." I go, "Exactly."*
>
> *I got really mad and I stopped hanging out in the dispatch office; I stopped slumming. What I didn't realize at the time was that this was the way that you started to work in the dispatch office. There was no training. When you were slumming in the office, if it got busy, you picked up the phone. Then the dispatcher would tell you what you were doing wrong, what other information they needed on the call, and you learned to answer the phones. Then when a shift became available, you became the phone answerer. And then a dispatcher.*

> *Essentially, although they were just "joking," it was really harassing me out of this opportunity. It turns out, [the person] who was hired two weeks after I was, was dispatching within the year, because he kept on slumming in the office.*

While this woman described her experience with sexual harassment as one which drove her out of the dispatch office and prevented her from receiving the necessary training to become a dispatcher, another woman, below, discussed how her fear of harassment forced her to curtail her after-hours activities. Specifically, she described her reluctance to go out with male co-workers after work in order to avoid sending a message that some would read as availability. She expressed her belief that these precautions and concerns would not be necessary if she were labeled "lesbian":

> *I did feel intimidated, sometimes. There was one situation that I thought was really out of hand, in that, one of the dispatchers [wouldn't stop harassing her]. Well, a lot of times if you're just nice, and you're thought of as straight, you open yourself up to being harassed. Sometimes I'm very reluctant to [go out with male co-workers after work] because I don't want it to be interpreted the wrong way.*

Thus, in order to avoid sexual harassment, this driver would seldom go out after work with her male co-workers. Withdrawal from the sexually harassing work area that results in those women missing promotion or training opportunities has been documented by other researchers (e.g., Paap 2006; Yount 1991).

Importantly for this study, withdrawal from the work area and mixed-sex socializing meant that the women at Co-op Cab did not develop friendships with many of the men in the company. This directly affected their dispute resolution options because all but one of the worker-managers were men. Without some social connections to the managers, women could not engage in informal dispute resolution, and only had the option of the formal grievance procedure.

In contrast to the heterosexual-labeled women discussed above, the women who were labeled as lesbian did not perceive sexual harassment as an issue at Co-op Cab. The statement below is characteristic of women who were labeled "lesbian":

> *My experience for the most part has been fine. People showed me*
> *respect, were courteous. Stuff like that ... I feel we have a good place in*
> *terms of harassment and discrimination. It depends on the person and*
> *the events ... I think the incidents are few and far between and I think*
> *the incidents are dealt with very quickly and fairly. Men and women*
> *get along pretty ok, I mean, we're not working in a utopia.*

Like the other lesbian-labeled women, this woman did not feel that she had been the target of sexual harassment.

In addition to the consensus on the lower rate of sexual harassment toward lesbian-labeled workers, all women interviewed indicated that men had noticeably less contact of any kind with those women they labeled lesbian. One woman who, having joined shortly after the co-op had formed, was the woman with the longest tenure, believed that merely deciding how to relate to their lesbian-labeled co-workers was difficult for many men:

> *I think it's a challenge for a lot of the men at work to figure out how*
> *to interact with me. I would imagine that the way that they feel weird*
> *about it is a little less exhausting to them than it was to me when I*
> *started working there and I was trying figure out how to deal with*
> *being with all these men.*

Perhaps as a result of this difficulty, many men at the cab company opted to avoid contact with their lesbian-labeled co-workers.

When the men interviewed (all of whom self-identified as heterosexual) discussed their interactions with the co-workers they labeled as lesbian, they all described having very limited contact with them. Some of the men's comments merely alluded to a gender split in the socializing at the cab company; however, other men, like the driver quoted below, discussed actively avoiding this group of women. He believed it was somehow better if the women he labeled as lesbian could be avoided. Like all but two men in this study, this man expressed fear of inadvertently offending others at the Co-op Cab. He believed that by avoiding lesbian-labeled women altogether he could avoid the risk of giving offense:

> *Well, so many women are lesbians that you really have to be careful. If*
> *you're not used to dealing with lesbians, you have to watch yourself.*
> *Sort of keep your distance. 'Cause you don't want to get them all upset*
> *with you, you know? I mean, who they are is ok and everything, and so*

you don't want to do something that would be misunderstood. 'Cause,
I mean, that's a lot of women who'd be mad at you.

This man's "solution" of simply avoiding lesbian co-workers was shared by many men at the company. This strategy of avoidance meant that one portion of the female workforce at the cab company, those women labeled lesbian, were kept from having much contact with the men at the co-op.

These two patterns of interaction meant that women—of either label—had less interaction with the majority group of the co-op and the group which comprised the managers: the men. The groups labeled lesbian were avoided and the women labeled heterosexual, although not avoided by their male co-workers in the way the lesbian-labeled workers were, instead were sometimes sexually harassed, and so they, themselves, deliberately avoided some or all of the men at the company. Thus, both groups of women, whether labeled lesbian or heterosexual, experienced fewer dispute resolution options compared to the men: the women relied exclusively on the formal grievance procedure while the men could choose between formal and informal resolution.

Discussion

The insiders—Co-op Cab men and Organix Co-op middle-class white workers—envisioned grievance strategies that seldom included the formal grievance processes, anticipating resolving differences through informal means, and only using the formal processes as a last resort. These "insiders" experienced greater "trust," "neutrality," and "standing" so that even in informal settings they perceived a "level playing field" (Tyler and Lind 2000: 76). The "insiders" felt part of the "family," or informal networks, giving them the option of using informal dispute resolution to achieve justice for themselves, but they also had a duty to not violate this loyalty to the social network by resorting to the formal processes. Thus, while it might appear that the informal route advantages the insiders in day-to-day grievance resolution strategies, the need to avoid the formal process meant these workers might not experience more options than their non-insider co-workers. However, if insiders needed to and felt sufficiently out of "group mode" already, they could resort to the formal grievance system, while their non-insider co-workers could not opt, no matter how desperate, for informal grievance resolution.

The insiders' hesitance to use the formal grievance procedures does not mean that they regarded the formal process as unimportant. Men and women at Co-op Cab and nearly everyone at Organix Co-op mentioned pride in this democratic aspect of the co-operative. For the insiders, the formal grievance procedures provided more symbolic value than instrumental, in that these procedures acquired an "immediate intrinsic significance ... oriented less to behavioral consequences as a means to a fixed end ... a gesture important in itself" (Gusfield 1967). However, for the others the formal grievance procedures held instrumental importance because their actual use had direct influence on how women approached grievances.

Since women at Co-op Cab and working-class and non-white workers at Organix Co-op lacked access to the social networks that allowed for informal dispute resolution, they only used the formal dispute resolution procedures. They believed that they would not receive procedural justice from the co-operative if they dealt with the worker-managers informally. However, most maintained confidence in the procedural justice possible through the formal grievance procedures. Even workers who lacked "trust" and doubted the "neutrality" of the grievance procedures believed they had sufficiently adequate levels of "standing" that they could have confidence in the appropriateness of using the formal procedures. As Tyler and Lind's theory of distributive and procedural justice predicts, non-insiders also expressed greater confidence than the insiders in the distributive justice possible from formal grievance procedures, where they believed they would receive more procedural justice than from informal negotiations with worker-managers and others.

Additionally, the formal grievance procedures also offered some protections not available through informal resolution: the formal setting allows an advocate to represent the worker, affording a level of distance between the grievant and the defending manager (Grillo 1991). In addition, if the grievant wins the appeal, they receive formal recognition acknowledging the management's error and unjust treatment. This benefits the individual grievants by publicly reaffirming their positions. Formal grievances also educate other workers since formal grievance procedures include posting summaries of all grievance decisions in the public break rooms. In contrast, if a worker and their supervisor resolve a grievance informally, the public gains little knowledge, if any (Edelman, Erlanger and Lande 1993).

Other scholars have shown that informal dispute resolution often disadvantages the less powerful party, while formal hearings can level an otherwise uneven playing field (e.g., Abel 1982; Crenshaw 1988; Delgado et al. 1985; Edelman, Erlanger and Lande 1993; Galanter 1974; Grillo 1991; Lazerson 1982; Sarat 1990; Silbey and Sarat 1989). Women at Co-op Cab and working-class non-white members at Organix Co-op held less power and so, in order to receive procedural justice, they needed to engage the formal processes. The formal grievance procedures provided many guarantees that they might not have if they tried to resolve issues informally; the formal process guaranteed that their side would be heard, that they could involve a third-party advocate to provide emotional distancing, that their case would be dealt with in a timely fashion, and that they would ultimately receive a clear answer to their grievance. In this way, formality provided them with protections that their less powerful status could not through informal negotiations. By invoking their right to a formal hearing, the women achieved procedural justice and gained some measure of equality despite their exclusion from the insiders' network.

Both women and men attributed their anticipated grievance resolution strategy—formal and informal respectively—partly to the identity of their workplace as a worker co-operative. For example, at Co-op Cab women said that the formal empowerment derived from co-operative ideology and shared ownership enabled them to raise formal grievances; men at the co-operative felt that these same elements allowed them greater access to worker-supervisors, thereby permitting them a choice of venue—informal or formal—to resolve their grievances. Additionally, however, because men operate in a "group mode" (Tyler and Lind 2000), some men felt pressure to avoid formal resolution, leaving them effectively with only one option also: informal resolution.

Tyler and Lind suggest that a significant part of people's evaluation of grievance resolution concerns their relationship to the social group: "If procedures are fair, ... people can feel secure about the long-term gains from group membership" (Tyler and Lind 2000: 76). People then hinge much of their social identity on having that group membership. This fear of exclusion is more important than the loss of any specific desired outcome (Tyler and Lind 2000). The official membership in the co-operative was very important for the workers at Co-op Cab and Organix Co-op. As worker co-operatives, these workplaces held greater significance than simply a place to work; they were also demonstrations of personally held ideologies, reflecting who their members were and what they believed. The importance of maintaining their confidence in their official standing was especially great because of the co-operative context. Some workers had deliberately sought out a co-operative work environment. That decision, in itself, represented a strong statement about their own identity. Other members discovered their co-op without ideology-driven searching, yet these workers, too, had developed a keen appreciation of the business as a co-operative, with their regard for the co-operative ideals growing as they continued at the company. Therefore, their social standing in the co-operative was important to both groups of workers in a way that would be quite different in a conventional workplace.

The non-white working-class members at Organix and the women workers at Co-op Cab often cited membership in the co-operative as key to enabling them to seek any grievance resolution at all. Although these workers spoke of lacking justice in informal interactions, they maintained their conviction that the co-operative's formal grievance procedures would provide procedural justice. Even the workers who lacked "trust" in the formal procedures and faith in its "neutrality" maintained sufficient confidence in their full status in the group "standing" (Tyler and Lind 2000). Thus, even though those workers expressed less confidence in the procedural justice possible through the formal grievance resolution procedures, they—like the rest of their non-insider co-workers—still anticipated using formal grievance strategies. Abandoning formal procedures would both cut off their only venue for resolving their grievances and negatively reflect on the co-operative and their status in it.

Conclusions

This chapter has explored how worker co-operatives sometimes struggle in their pursuit for a just workplace at which all members are equal. In particular, this chapter discussed how women cab drivers fared in the predominantly male Co-op Cab and how working-class and non-white members fared in the mostly middle-class white Organix Co-op. In both cases, these somewhat disempowered groups were still able to have their grievances addressed, but were more able to use formal means, while their male or middle-class or white peers felt equally able to resolve disputes formally or informally.

The insiders at both Co-op Cab and Organix Co-op also had greater social ties to the more powerful people in the company. At Co-op Cab all the worker-managers, except one, were men. Since the men at the cab company socialized with other male co-workers and the women socialized with other female co-workers, the men developed informal connections to the (male) worker-managers. This gave them access to resolving grievances informally, if they so chose, rather than going through the formal grievance procedures.

At Organix Co-op, no one group of workers comprised the worker-managers. However, the members who were from a middle-class background and were white were able to engage in informal dispute resolution that was not available to working-class and non-white workers. These "insiders" had greater connections to others in the co-operative and greater informal authority in the co-operative, enabling them to resolve their issues informally, and avoid the formal grievance procedure if they wished.

This demonstrates how the quest for equality that many of the co-operatives embark on can often be complicated. However, this also reveals how even those co-op members who only had one means of dispute resolution (formal routes) were nevertheless vastly better off than those employees at the conventional, hierarchical businesses where workers often talked of having confidence in no dispute resolution strategy. Those employees unable to address their workplace issues had to learn to tolerate their problems or quit their jobs. At the co-ops, despite the inequitable access to informal routes, no Co-op Cab or Organix Co-op member felt unable to resolve disputes effectively, one way or another.

Works Cited

Abel, R.L. (1982). The Contradictions of Informal Justice. In *The Politics of Informal Justice*, edited by R.L. Abel. New York: Academic Press.

Crenshaw, K. (1988). Race, Reform and Retrenchment: Transformation and Legitimation in Antidiscrimination Law. *Harvard Law Review* 101:1131–1387.

Delgado, R., Dunn, C., Brown, P., Lee, H. and Hubbert, D. (1985). Fairness and Formality: Minimizing the Risk of Prejudice in Alternative Dispute Resolution. *Wisconsin Law Review* 1985:585–629.

Edelman, L.B., Erlanger, H.S. and Lande, J. (1993). Internal Dispute Resolution: The Transformation of Civil Rights in the Workplace. *Law and Society Review* 27:497–534.

Galanter, M. (1974). Why the 'Haves' Come Out Ahead: Speculations on the Limits of Legal Change. *Law & Society Review* 9:95–127.

Grillo, T. (1991). The Mediation Alternative: Process Dangers for Women. *Yale Law Journal* 100:1545–1610.

Gusfield, J. (1967). "Moral Passage: The Symbolic Process in Public Designations of Deviance." *Social Problems* 15:175–188.

Hirschman, A.O. (1970). *Exit, Voice, and Loyalty: Responses to Declines in Firms, Organizations, and States*. Cambridge: Harvard University Press.

Hoffmann, E.A. (2005). Dispute Resolution in a Worker Co-operative: Formal Procedures and Procedural Justice. *Law & Society Review* 39:51–82.

Hoffmann, E.A. (2004). Selective Sexual Harassment: How the Labeling of Token Workers Can Produce Different Workplace Environments for Similar Groups of Women. *Law and Human Behavior: Special Issue on Employment and the Law* 28:29–45.

Lazerson, M.H. (1982). In the Halls of Justice, the Only Justice is in the Halls. in *The Politics of Informal Justice*, edited by R.L. Abel. New York: Academic Press.

Paap, K. (2006). *Working Construction: Why White Working-Class Men Put Themselves and the Labor Movement in Harm's Way*. Ithaca, NY, Cornell University Press: Industrial and Labor Relations Imprint.

Sarat, A. (1990). '... The Law is All Over': Power, Resistance and the Legal Consciousness of the Welfare Poor. *Yale Journal of Law & the Humanities* 2:343–379.

Schneider, B.E. (1982). Consciousness About Sexual Harassment Among Heterosexual and Lesbian Women Workers. *Journal of Social Issues* 38:75–98.

Silbey, S. and Sarat, A. (1989). Dispute Processing in Law and Legal Scholarship: From Institutional Critique to the Reconstruction of the Juridical Subject. *Denver University Law Review* 66:437–479.

Tyler, T.R. and Lind, E.A. (2000). Procedural Justice. pp. 65–92 in *Handbook of Justice Research in Law*, edited by J. Sanders and V.L. Hamilton. New York: Kluwer Academic/Plenum Publishers.

Welsh, S. and Gruber, J.E. (1999). Not Taking it any More: Women Who Report or File Complaints of Sexual Harassment. *Canadian Review of Sociology and Anthropology* 36:559–583.

Wright, E.O. (2010). *Envisioning Real Utopias*. New York: Verso.

Yount, K.R. (1991). Ladies, Flirts, and Tomboys: Strategies for Managing Sexual Harassment in an Underground Coal Mine. *Journal of Contemporary Ethnography* 19:396–422.

8

Lessons for the Rest of Us: The Co-operative Landscape[1]

The research reported in the foregoing chapters compared workplace dispute resolution strategies of workers at two very different types of companies: conventional, hierarchical businesses and worker co-operatives. As these examinations of Coal Co-operative, Co-op Cab, and Organix Co-op demonstrate, worker co-operatives can exist as successful financial alternatives to conventional organizations. As Pateman argued, in organizations that foster democratic participation, workers' activism will be greater (Pateman 1970). Indeed, each co-operative in this study emphasized democratic organization and encouraged workers' participation in the management of the organization. Through inclusion in work groups, serving on workers' councils, voting for members of the elected bodies (such as boards of directors), and attendance at regular membership meetings, these workers learned to be participatory members in a workplace democracy. The democratic participation in their workplaces affected the work lives of these co-op members in many ways.

Workplace Disputes

Disputes are difficult, often emotional, and time-consuming in whatever type of workplace they occur; no one relishes having problems at work. Yet, the greater the variety of choices workers have to address those problems, the better their work lives will be and the more efficient and successful their workplaces will become.

The research presented here demonstrates that the structure and ideology of co-operative organizations can have an effect on how employees resolve

---

1   Small portions of this chapter have appeared in Dispute Resolution in Co-operative and Hierarchical Worksites. (2006). *Advances in Industrial and Labor Relations* 15:35–66.

their workplace disputes. Rather than inhibiting grievances—workers placing their own needs behind their concern for the greater common good, as some literature suggests (Rothschild and Whitt 1986; Tucker 1999)—workers in co-operatives often had more options at their disposal for resolving workplace disputes than conventional employees in the same industry.

All three co-operatives featured in this book actively created grievance cultures that guided their members' naming of problems—naming, in particular, which responses were considered appropriate for either formal grievances or informal resolution. Co-op Cab most actively tried to teach new members the company's grievance culture: that bringing grievances was their right, and possibly even their duty. Co-op Cab did this through explicit new member orientations, and all the co-ops used member handbooks, active grievances, and informal discussions to educate members. This naming helped form the legal consciousness of the companies' members, establishing which dispute resolution strategies were appropriate in a given situation.

Despite the co-operatives' efforts to enable workers to successfully address their disputes and problems, some of the problems documented in conventional businesses still exist in the co-operatives. Co-operative members can encounter various barriers to mobilization and difficulties in negotiating various dispute resolution routes, as discussed in Chapter 2. Lower-status workers—such as the women employees at the taxicab company or the non-white or working-class workers at Organix—had greater difficulty building the informal network connections that make informal dispute resolution possible. Informal alliances, friendships, and contacts sustained outside the workplace are often hidden from the "official" organization. Therefore, co-operatives—and all organizations perhaps—should be attentive to any informal exclusion that would diminish access to unofficial sources of power in the organization since these exclusions affect workers' dispute resolution options. As the earlier chapters in this book have shown, perceptions of power and access influence workers' attitudes on resolving disputes in both informal and formal settings.

Dispute Resolution Strategies

Although all members of the worker co-operatives did not address their grievances in one single fashion, when it comes to dispute resolution strategies, a clear pattern exists—and it starkly contrasts with the pattern at the conventional, hierarchical businesses: Members of the co-ops consistently had more options for addressing their workplace disputes than their counterparts in the conventional companies. In each industry, members of the worker co-operatives described more dispute resolution options than their conventional-business counterparts. While co-op members often described having both formal and informal strategies at their disposal, their conventionally employed counterparts often mentioned one or the other. Additionally, employees in the more hierarchical businesses were more likely simply to adopt coping mechanisms ("toleration") rather than raise their grievances either formally or informally. Table 8.1 summarizes the percentage of workers at each business who discussed each dispute resolution strategy.

Table 8.1   **Dispute resolution strategies: percentages of employees who mentioned each dispute resolution strategy**

	Taxicab Industry		Whole Foods Industry		Coal Mining Industry	
	Private Taxi	Co-op Cab	HealthBite Distributors	Organix Co-op	Valley Colliery	Coal Co-operative
Formal Processes	14%	55%	0%	74%	90%	46%
Informal Processes	43%	60%	56%	69%	3%	92%
Toleration	36%	5%	61%	29%	11%	3%
Exit	36%	20%	17%	23%	0%	0%

Percentages sum to greater than 100 percent in some cases because the categories are not exclusive; some interviewees mentioned more than one dispute resolution strategy.

Note: a "no response" category does not exist. All interviewees provided at least one strategy.

Formal and Informal Processes

COAL MINING

Miners in the more hierarchical mine, Valley Colliery, mostly described resolving disputes formally (90 percent). They explained that informal means were not effective and that they rarely attempted them. Many employees, such as the one quoted below, explained that raising formal grievances was their only avenue, because managers refused to engage in informal dispute resolution: "They'd *tell* you rather than ask you," one of the control room workers explained. "There was no talking to them."

Another miner explained that the response to a dispute could be a walkout by the miners or a lockout by the management—both extreme forms of formal action and exercises in official power. For example, one worker said, if management "couldn't have their own way, they'd send the men home."

In contrast, the members of Coal Co-operative spoke of their ability to resolve disputes through informal means (92 percent) and formal grievances (46 percent) both. Many issues they had only dealt with formally before the conversion to a co-operative could now be handled informally. One miner, who had been at the mine for seven years before the worker buy-out, said he recently took up the issue of leaving unfinished work over a weekend with a manager: "Obviously, he's had a word with my foreman and I sorted it out with the foreman," he explained. "If you don't bring the point up, it'll just keep on happening."

The availability of informal means did not mean that the formal procedures were abandoned. Indeed, workers at Coal Co-operative also used formal grievance procedures (46 percent). For example, one electrician spoke of how it was now acceptable to raise formal grievances on issues that would not have been deemed sufficiently important or appropriate under British Coal's management. For example, he brought a formal grievance regarding the quality of toilet paper (the managers used to have higher quality toilet paper than the workers): "It matters," he said, "the things like that, silly little things. It says 'I'm no better than that manager over there, and he's no better than me.'"

Miners also used formal grievances to address safety concerns, since certain safety risks, if left unattended, could lead to injury, death, or economic loss for the mine.

TAXICAB DRIVING

In contrast to the coal industry—in which the conventional mine workers could resolve grievances formally but not informally, while those in the co-operative mine could raise disputes both formally and informally—workers in the more hierarchical taxicab company, Private Taxi, explained that they could raise some disputes informally (43 percent). But Private Taxi employees rarely mentioned formal procedures among their dispute resolution strategies

(14 percent). A Private Taxi driver explained that employees tried whatever means they could, with whomever they could, to attempt to resolve grievances informally: "Everyone goes to whoever they think they're going to get some satisfaction from," he said.

Each employee at Private Taxi had to negotiate on his or her own, seeking informal resolution without predictable outcomes. Often, this dynamic led many employees to simply learn to tolerate problems (36 percent), rather than attempting either formal or informal resolution, as discussed later.

While the Private Taxi workers had barely one means of resolving grievances, the members at Co-op Cab spoke of using both formal (55 percent) and informal ways (60 percent) of resolving workplace disputes. Many members explained that a key advantage to being part of a worker co-operative was that formal grievances were more socially acceptable and easier to raise: "People aren't afraid to bring grievances if they feel they've got one," said one woman who had been at Co-op Cab for about two years. "I think there's sort of a sense that there's few jobs where you have that opportunity, so make the most of it."

One driver and dispatcher who had also worked at Co-op Cab for about two years said he had never had a dispute that he couldn't resolve informally; he never had the need to use the formal grievance procedures: "I talk to a lot of people. If I have a problem, I can talk to someone and work it out," he explained.

His statement is typical of most men at Co-op Cab. Men generally said they were comfortable raising grievances formally or informally, but usually preferred informal routes.

In contrast, many women at Co-op did not feel comfortable using informal routes. Although they did not feel they had access to informal options, the women were comfortable with, anticipated using, and had used their co-operative's formal grievance procedures. Much of this dynamic was due to the somewhat sex-segregated socializing at the cab co-operative and the fact that most of the worker-managers, who had the power to informally negotiate disputes, were men. This created an environment in which the women lacked the social networks to enable them to resolve grievances informally (Hoffmann 2004; Hoffmann 2005).

Nevertheless, although not all members of Co-op Cab were able to use both formal and informal means, both strategies for dispute resolution were used in the co-operative.

FOOD DISTRIBUTION

Members of Organix Co-op also described both formal (74 percent) and informal dispute resolution strategies (69 percent). For example, one worker described a recent formal grievance:

> *Someone kept moving some equipment I needed. He'd put it away, so it was more convenient for his work, but then I'd have to get it back and that always put me behind. I tried to get him to change, but, in the end, I [filed a grievance against him].*

Others preferred to resolve disputes through informal routes: "I tend to not go to the meetings," said one long-time member of Organix Co-op. "I like to chat things up in the pub. That's just the way I like to do it."

As at Co-op Cab, some members of Organix Co-op were more able to use both formal and informal routes than others. Rather than falling along gender lines, at Organix, members who felt less able to resolve grievances informally were less formally educated, of lower-class status, and were non-white. However, these less-empowered members, like the women at Co-op Cab, still were able to bring formal grievances. Nevertheless, despite this inequitable access to informal routes, no Organix Co-op member felt unable to resolve disputes effectively, one way or another, in contrast to workers at HealthBite, the more hierarchical food distribution company. At HealthBite, most workers felt that neither option was very promising.

Employees at HealthBite were similar to the employees in the hierarchical taxicab company who most anticipated informal dispute resolution options (56 percent). In fact, the employees at HealthBite relied even more exclusively on informal routes, with no one (0 percent) anticipating using the formal dispute mechanisms that were available at the company. Indeed, the formal procedures were not an option that many considered, and those who did consider them thought they were not worthwhile. In practice, employees at HealthBite were left to their own informal strategies if they wanted to resolve problems.

Many employees felt unable to raise grievances formally or informally. These workers often developed ways of coping with their problems at work, rather than trying to resolve them formally or informally. This is discussed in the following section.

Toleration

A number of workers developed toleration strategies to handle workplace disputes (Hoffmann 2006). Since toleration strategies do not involve actually addressing the disputes at hand, they technically are not dispute resolution strategies. Nevertheless, these toleration strategies did provide ways for workers to continue in their workplaces by learning to cope with various problems. Sometimes the toleration strategy involved simply saying nothing and swallowing one's aggravation; while other times workers voiced their frustrations, but only to uninvolved co-workers.

In each industry, employees at the more hierarchical businesses were more likely to talk about dispute strategies that involved toleration (see Table 8.1). Workers who could not or would not raise their disputes either formally or informally—and who wished to remain at the organization—were left in the position of having to learn to tolerate the problems.

COAL MINING

Coal miners were some of the least likely to mention toleration strategies. Unlike the workers at the other conventionally owned businesses, the employees at Valley Colliery seldom mentioned toleration (11 percent). This is because they were part of the very active NUM miners' union. Similarly, at the co-operative mine, only a tiny fraction (3 percent) mentioned toleration. As discussed above, the miners were more likely to bring their grievances to their union representatives, rather than learning to quietly tolerate problems (Hoffmann 2001; Hoffmann 2006).

TAXICAB DRIVING

Many workers who had become frustrated with past attempts to address grievances developed coping strategies and learned ways to adapt to various problems rather than resolve them. At Private Taxi, 36 percent talked of using toleration strategies for dealing with grievances, but only 5 percent of members of Co-op Cab did. An example of the toleration strategy in the cab industry comes from this veteran cab driver at Private Taxi, who explains how he tried to "just stay real calm" and not let problems bother him: "I know it ain't gonna do no good to complain. You can't get uptight about it." Like many of his co-workers, this driver was proud of his ability to ignore potential disputes.

Often, workers doubted their managers would be responsive to attempts to resolve their grievances, formal or informal, as this Private Taxi cab driver explains below:

> Unfair sh*t is always going to happen. That's why it's good to go out the airport. When you're waiting for rides at the airport, you can hang out with other drivers and complain about the bad call you got from that dispatcher, or how you didn't get the shift you were supposed to, or how some other driver cheated you out of a ride. You get to get all that stuff out, off your chest. And that's real good to do, because that's usually all you can do.

Many employees in the hierarchical cab company and the conventional food distribution company believed management would resist their attempts to address workplace disputes; therefore they were resigned to simply tolerate their unraised grievances.

FOOD DISTRIBUTION

At Healthbite, a majority of workers (61 percent) mentioned toleration strategies for dealing with problems in the workplace, although only 29 percent at Organix Co-op. For example, an employee at HealthBite explained that his preferred path was often to do nothing: "You can't have too thin a skin. You can't complain all the time," he said. "Nothing's perfect. Just focus on what you're doing and get on with it." Many similarly situated employees shared this strategy of pushing past problems to accomplish their work despite potential disputes.

Exiting

Quitting was an important strategy for some workers. Particularly at the conventional, hierarchical businesses, exit offered a way to avoid an outright confrontation and a means for escaping workplace disputes if a confrontation failed to produce the desired results. However, exit is a complicated dispute resolution strategy. It demands forfeiting one's job, with all of the financial hardship that implies. It also means putting time and effort into locating another job, which may or may not be as attractive as the current job—something many workers considered.

COAL MINING

Remarkably, not one miner (0 percent) at either mine mentioned exit—quitting—as a possible way to resolve workplace conflicts in our discussions of dispute resolution strategies.

This is likely due to the high exit and entry costs for the deep-pit mining industry, making quitting to resolve disputes nearly unthinkable. Additionally, for many of the workers, being a miner was more than simply a job; it was a key part of their identities (Hoffmann 2001; Hoffmann 2006).

Many miners were concerned about preserving their jobs and keeping the mine open, since many deep-pit mines in the United Kingdom had already been closed. These miners expressed anxiety not with simply keeping their jobs, but in keeping *these* jobs. Many of them had fathers and grandfathers who had been deep-pit coal miners. For them, deep-pit mining was part of their heritage. As one miner said, "They've been brought up on coal mining … probably the conversation in their home has been about coal mining and in the pub on Saturday and the club on Saturday." Since the workers both at Coal Co-operative and Valley Colliery saw their jobs as precious commodities, it is not surprising that no one mentioned leaving.

In fact, Hirschman (1970) says that the amount of loyalty often depends on a person's identification with the organization or group. Dowding et al. elaborate on this aspect of Hirschman's thesis, writing, "[A] person may feel great loyalty to the firm for which she works, despite considering its current management to be fools and buffoons ruining the organization" (Dowding et al. 2000: 447). Indeed, the workers at both of the coal mines strongly identified with their particular mine. Leaving the organization would have meant changing their identity and reconceptualizing who they were. Thus, the exit costs were extremely high for both groups of miners, resulting in no one considering "exit" as a possible dispute resolution strategy.

Additionally, as mentioned earlier in the descriptions of the mines, the miners who were forced to take factory jobs (the only other jobs available) between the time of the mine closing and its reopening as a co-operative detested the factory work. Several of them stated that they would rather have no job than have to return to factory work. The available factory work was small-scale assembly of computer parts—which more than one miner referred to as "dainty women's work." In many ways, the only way to maintain their identities, particularly their masculine identities (Cheng 1996; Connell 1995), was to work in the mines.

Moreover, the mining co-operative also had the highest entry costs, requiring a $13,000 buy-in by each worker. Therefore, it makes sense that members of the co-operative would be even more reluctant than their conventional organization counterparts to exit—although a rate lower than zero does not exist to quantify this.

TAXICAB DRIVING

Thirty-six percent of Private Taxi employees mentioned exiting as a way of addressing workplace disputes, while only 20 percent of Co-op Cab workers did. As one 24-year-old Private Taxi driver put it, "If it gets to be too much, quit. I like it, but I could leave any time, too, especially if I was having some kind of problem."

However, even though many conditions were similar, workers at Co-op Cab were less likely to talk about quitting. Not only did a smaller percentage of workers at Co-op Cab discuss exiting, but, when they did, they did not embrace a "we can always quit" approach and rarely mentioned exiting as a way to address workplace problems.

FOOD DISTRIBUTION

Although workers at both HealthBite and Organic Co-op mentioned leaving, the workers' motivations for considering quitting were quite dissimilar. The workers at HealthBite who mentioned "exit" as a strategy (17 percent) felt that quitting would be an easy option if they found themselves unhappy at their jobs because such jobs are easily replaced.

However, workers at Organix Co-op (23 percent) explained that they would quit if they felt betrayed by the co-operative—not because they could easily find another similar job. For example, one woman said that if she felt sufficiently upset to bring a grievance, she would probably leave rather than raise the formal grievance, saying, "I'd just feel that I'd been let down too badly."

Scholars who study exiting strategies assert that "those [workers] who care the *most* who would be the most active, reliable, and creative agents of voice are, for that very reason, also those who are apparently likely to exit first in cases of deterioration [emphasis in original]" (Hirschman 1970: 47). With this in mind, it is interesting to note that Organix Co-op, the co-op with the greatest co-operative ideological zeal (see earlier descriptions of businesses), is also the co-op where members report more exit strategies: for these workers, if the co-operative adopted "wrongful" policies, or made poor decisions that they felt compromised the co-operative's integrity, they would consider quitting—not as a way to resolve disputes, but as a form of protest to register their disgust.

Implications for Improving the Workplace

Co-operatives are not so substantially different from their conventional counterparts in several important ways. They all still must turn a profit, obey labor laws and other laws and rules, and survive in the market. Some might argue, in fact, that worker co-operatives are actually the epitome of the free enterprise system. In fact, worker co-operatives do offer a number of suggestions for conventional businesses.

The results of this study hold great promise for improving the workplace. I have focused on dispute resolution behavior in worker co-operatives, but its results also suggest improvements for other aspects of work life. The organizations appearing in this book demonstrate that co-operative organization affects workplace disputes, which are often the most disruptive and difficult parts of employees' work. Even though it is doubtful that an established company would suddenly embrace mutual ownership, shared management, and worker equality, it is possible for mainstream businesses to incorporate various aspects of co-operatives.

For example, a number of businesses have programs that allow employees to more easily purchase or earn stock in their company. Some organizations have begun Employee Stock Ownership Plans (ESOPs), which facilitate employees gaining stock in their workplaces. Alternatively, some companies engage in profit sharing with their workers. This can occur after each quarter, at the year's end, or after completion of specific projects.

Even without any financial changes, conventional organizations can increase the level of worker input into managerial decisions. Businesses can create self-management groups as one method of increasing the amount of worker input; these efforts can be project-specific or ongoing. Other businesses allow worker input (without actually ceding any management control) through worker-management discussions and open debates, with the management still responsible for making final decisions. Conversely, workers can have some organizational-level control—without the time-consuming worker-management meetings of most worker co-operatives—by giving each employee a vote, whether they own stock or not; this allows employees to help elect members of their organization's board of directors and to vote on other decisions.

Without radically restructuring power relations, efforts by businesses to embrace a doctrine of equality could seem disingenuous. However, corporations could apply some strategies for heightening workers' feelings of worth and "standing" within the organization. The most direct way would be by increasing workplace due process through appeals procedures, worker advocates and ombudsmen, and transparent and accessible grievance procedures. Union representation could accomplish much of this, but organizations could implement these changes even in non-union businesses. In fact, simply giving workers the financial participation or increased worker input, as discussed above, could increase worker status and create a stable, satisfied workforce.

One of the most important differences for workers in co-operatives is that members of the co-operatives have more avenues to resolve their disputes. The data in this study confirm many of the predictions from the scholarly literature. The study demonstrates that co-operative structure and ideology can have a profound impact on the members' dispute resolution strategies, enabling them to have more options than their counterparts in conventional businesses. In the coal mining industry, miners at the conventionally organized mine had only formal routes through which to resolve their disputes, while those at the co-operative mine could use both formal or informal avenues. In the taxicab industry, employees at the conventional company most often anticipated resolving disputes informally—and even then, could only occasionally engage in dispute resolution at all. In contrast, members of the taxicab co-operative resolved disputes both formally and informally. In the food distribution industry, workers at the conventional company rarely tried to resolve their disputes—more often relying on their own toleration strategies; but when they did attempt dispute resolution, they worked informally rather than through formal mechanisms. Their counterparts in the worker co-operative were more able to resolve disputes through both formal and informal means.

These findings also strengthen the contention that organizations can work well without an extensive hierarchical power structure, questioning the assertions of many scholars over the last 80 years (Hannan and Freeman 1989; Lipset, Trow, and Coleman 1956; Michels 1962; Weber 1946). While this is interesting at a theoretical level, it also is important on an applied level. These findings lend strength to organizational innovations that call for greater employee control of, input into, and ownership of their work. While few businesses are likely to reorganize themselves into worker co-operatives, many may consider various plans of heightened worker involvement and ownership, but then might dismiss such plans as impractical. This research lends credence to these potential workplace innovations.

This research also offers some tentative implications for co-operative interdependence, when workers expect each person to work hard toward the shared goals; therefore, interdependent workers are more likely to exchange information and support each other and to have stronger interpersonal relationships (Tjosvold, Morishima, and Belsheim 1999). Members of the co-ops were clearly engaged in what the scholarship in this area describes as co-operative interdependence. These co-op workers—although they would disagree sometimes on the specifics of managing the day-to-day activities of the co-operatives—were united in wanting the co-operatives to succeed. The realization of co-operative members' shared goals seemed to have the dual effect of enabling members to speak up when they perceived a problem as well as reducing the need to silently tolerate problems or develop coping skills.

Such findings can be applied to non-cooperative, conventional workplaces in that a workplace might facilitate management and workers acknowledging shared goals and working together to meet those goals. Even without creating shared profits, much less shared ownership, conventional workplaces might still be able to achieve co-operative interdependence and, therefore, benefit from reduced turnover, higher morale, and greater contributions regarding how to improve the organizations.

This study has also demonstrated that workers in co-operatives did not experience as many barriers to dispute resolution as did comparable employees in conventional businesses within the same industries. The employees of the conventional businesses experienced multiple barriers to resolving disputes, similar to those documented by past studies of hierarchical businesses (Bumiller 1988; Edelman, Erlanger, and Lande 1993). Unlike most studies of dispute resolution, which are situated within conventional, hierarchical organizations, this study revealed that members of co-operatives were less likely to see a grievance as "unwinnable" (Bumiller 1988) or be stymied by their individual disputant status (Galanter 1974).

The unique privilege of working in a co-operative was symbolized for many by the monetary costs that members had to pay to join the co-operatives. At Coal Co-operative, workers had to buy in with cash in hand before they could begin a day of work. This sometimes required substantial loans from family, friends, or financial institutions. In the case of Organix and Co-op Cab, workers had to put in a set number of hours at a lower wage until they had earned equity in the company, with part of their wages going, unseen, toward buying into the co-op. Once they had worked enough hours, they became full voting and owning members. The literal buying-in that the co-operatives required had both practical and emotional components. Only the committed would go through the initial financial hardship buying-in required, so joining the worker co-operatives inherently involved a higher level of intentionality as well as possibly a certain amount of self-selection. It also was a concrete way members could view their place in the company in very tangible terms, for example, "For this job, I paid $8,000." It highlighted how these jobs had a greater worth than jobs they could just walk into, even when the jobs at the co-operatives seemed mired in the same mundane, annoying aspects of everyday work.

Many workers spoke of how being owners offered them a different relationship to their company. Some spoke of how they took pride in small acts of thrift for the good of the company, such as the Organix worker who said she always tried to pick up as many paper clips off the floor as possible to prevent them from being swept up and thrown away at the end of the day. Others spoke about how the knowledge that their company was "theirs" overrode negative feelings that might be part of any work day anywhere – such as resistance to working on one of the first warm days of spring, to use an example from a worker at Co-op Cab, which was located in the upper Midwest, known for its long, bitter cold winters.

The shared involvement in management decisions, also, was important to co-op members. Workers at all three companies spoke of the ways this shared involvement affected the ways their own work was organized. The coal miners spoke of this most passionately, describing how in pre-cooperative days the miners would be sent into conditions that they knew were at best underproductive, or, at worst dangerous and unsafe, yet mine managers did not consider their objections. Now, in each co-operative examined in this book, the people doing the jobs provided input into how those jobs would be run, and large-scale decisions could be addressed through democratic processes. Although all the co-operatives still had managers, the hierarchies were radically flattened, and the managers supervised within narrow ranges of authority: this involvement in managerial decision-making helped workers feel greater emotional ties to their businesses. Indeed, many workers spoke of their companies as families—sometimes ones where members disagreed or squabbled, but families, with affection and loyalty, nonetheless.

Mainstream, conventional businesses have experimented with a variety of worker-involvement schemes. Programs such as Total Quality Management (TQM), employee-management circles, the inclusion of employees on various committees, and the range of union representation have all attempted to give workers some level of input into management decisions. Some research indicates that such programs may empower employees and can achieve a higher level of worker "buy-in" emotionally. However, it is unclear if these worker-involvement schemes can actually achieve the level that the worker co-operatives did.

Each worker co-operative strove for equality among co-operative members; yet, achieving it demanded more than simply sharing decision-making and co-owning stock. The co-ops tried to create workplaces of equality through attention to day-to-day details, administrative procedures, and organizational information and access. Day-to-day, workers experienced a great deal of empowerment in terms of work schedules and when and how to do assigned tasks. When work was done in groups, such as at Organix, the group could collectively make these decisions. Administratively, equality was put into practice by giving each person a seat, a vote, and a voice (although not all would choose to speak) at meetings. Importantly, although perhaps not as obviously demonstrated, all members had access to information about the businesses. Questions on the success of certain operations, revenue, and other similar concerns could be brought to the group or person responsible for that information, either publicly at co-op meetings or privately.

Many members of co-operatives were aware that worker activism was not automatic. New workers often had to learn how to be active members of a co-operative, as Pateman's research asserts (Pateman 1970). Co-operative members were conscious of what they saw as the necessary ideological transition from being an employee to being a worker-owner. Even though for many, part of the motivation for joining co-operatives was the desire for a different kind of workplace, they acknowledged that people tend to revert to the type of work situation with which they are most familiar. Each co-operative had various ways to educate its members. All co-operatives had handbooks and new-member materials that explained the privileges, duties, and responsibilities of membership. Co-op Cab and Organix had new-member orientations, and Organix had a mentor program for new members. The following quote from a woman at the taxicab co-operative illustrates this induction process:

> We're also working on a position called head training coordinator ... that will make people who are coming in who aren't from a union shop background or a co-operative background get the idea that if they don't like something they don't have to put up with it just because they like their job. There is probably a reason why they don't like it and it could be fixed. I don't think people come in understanding that they can speak their minds without being retaliated against.

In addition to these formal means, informal education and re-education occurred in daily personal interactions and at meetings and other group settings. For example, at Coal Co-operative, members easily and articulately discussed what it meant to be a member of a co-operative around the dining tables at the canteen. At one Co-op Cab Workers' Council hearing I attended, the worker who had brought the grievance spoke about what she felt were the key elements of a worker co-operative, generating discussion among the members. At Organix meetings I attended, workers vigorously debated which actions by the organization would be the most "true" to the co-operative ideology.

Despite all these efforts toward equality and involvement, not all members of co-operatives experienced greater opportunities for dispute resolution and participation. Interestingly, in two of the three co-operatives, a portion of the members was unable to utilize *both* formal and informal routes of dispute resolutions. The women at Co-op Cab and the working-class, non-white members of Organix Co-op were not as able as their co-workers to resolve grievances informally. While the co-operative structure and ideology enabled them to use the formal grievance procedures, their difference in social status from their "insider" co-workers left them with less access to the informal power and networks necessary to resolve grievances informally. Although the demographics of the marginalized groups were different between the two co-operatives, this finding suggests that power structures, such as class and gender, which are present in the larger society, still have a serious impact on the experiences of co-operative workers.

This presents an important reminder to conventional and co-operative businesses alike. Even when various structural changes are made to heighten equality among workers, one must still be aware that some sub-groups might not be able to achieve that full equality. Substantial awareness of differences among workers and the possible barriers that those differences may cause would be essential to creating a truly egalitarian workplace.

Works Cited

Bumiller, K. (1988). *The Civil Rights Society: The Social Construction of Victims*. Baltimore: The John Hopkins University Press.

Cheng, C. (1996). *Masculinities in Organizations*. Thousand Oaks: Sage Publications.

Connell, R.W. (1995). *Masculinities*. Berkeley: University of California Press.

Dowding, K., John, P., Mergoupis, T. and Van Vugt, M. (2000). Exit, Voice and Loyalty: Analytic and Empirical Developments. *European Journal of Political Research* 37:469–495.

Edelman, L.B., Erlanger, H.S. and Lande, J. (1993). Internal Dispute Resolution: The Transformation of Civil Rights in the Workplace. *Law and Society Review* 27:497–534.

Galanter, M. (1974). Why the 'Haves' Come Out Ahead: Speculations on the Limits of Legal Change. *Law & Society Review* 9:95–127.

Hannan, M.T. and Freeman, J. (1989). *Organizational Ecology*. Cambridge: Harvard University Press.

Hirschman, A.O. (1970). *Exit, Voice, and Loyalty: Responses to Declines in Firms, Organizations, and States*. Cambridge: Harvard University Press.

Hoffmann, E.A. (2001). Confrontations and Compromise: Dispute Resolution at a Worker Co-operative Coal Mine. *Law & Social Inquiry* 26:555–596.

Hoffmann, E. (2004). Selective Sexual Harassment: How the Labeling of Token Workers Can Produce Different Workplace Environments for Similar Groups of Women. *Law and Human Behavior* 28:29–45.

Hoffmann, E. (2005). Dispute Resolution in a Worker Co-operative: Formal Procedures and Procedural Justice.' *Law & Society Review* 39:51–82.

Hoffmann, E. (2006). Exit and Voice: Organizational Loyalty and Dispute Resolution Strategies. *Social Forces* 84:2313–2330.

Lipset, S.M., Trow, M.A. and Coleman, J.S. (1956). *Union Democracy*. New York: Free Press.

Michels, R. (1962). *Political Parties*. Translated by E. Paul and C. Paul. New York: The Crowell-Collier Publishing Company.

Pateman, C. (1970). *Participation and Democratic Theory*. London: Cambridge University Press.

Rothschild, J. and Whitt, J.A. (1986). *The Co-operative Workplace: Potentials and Dilemmas of Organizational Democracy and Participation*. Cambridge: Cambridge University Press.

Tjosvold, D., Morishima, M. and Belsheim, J.A. (1999). Complaint Handling on the Shop Floor: Co-operative Relationships and Open-Minded Strategies. *The International Journal of Conflict Management* 10:45–68.

Tucker, J. (1999). *The Therapeutic Corporation*. New York: Oxford University Press.

Weber, M. (1946). *From Max Weber: Essays in Sociology*. Translated by H. Gerth and C.W. Mills. New York: Oxford University Press.

Appendix: Methodology for Author's Research

I used the comparative case method to explore dispute resolution strategies and attitudes (Ragin 1987). I interviewed and observed workers in three industries: coal mining, taxicab driving, and organic food distribution, returning to each site several times. Within each industry, I studied a worker co-operative and a matched conventional business. The industries in this study offered a range of workplace cultures, gender balances, and business objectives. I visited each business two or three times, observing as well as interviewing workers and achieving variation in interviewees on many dimensions. The duration of the visits ranged from a few days to two weeks. I did not use any survey instruments since many of the questions I asked responded to the interviewees' statements.

One Mine/Two Systems

Valley Colliery and Coal Co-operative were "deep-pit" mines, meaning deep underground mining, as opposed to strip mining. The two coal mines in this study were the same physical mine under two different systems of ownership and management. I visited the mine a total of three times. I conducted the first two sets of interviews several years after the reopening of the mine as a co-operative. Therefore, since these miners were only interviewed after the conversion of the mine into a co-operative, some of the data rely on their recollections of the organization three years earlier, when British Coal owned the mine. However, this situation allowed the miners to provide important insights regarding workers' attitudes toward raising grievances under both ownership situations. Moreover, by studying the same company, this study avoids many comparability problems that arise from comparisons of two or more companies, such as variation in the composition of the workforce, challenges at separate work sites, and dissimilar institutional histories.

I returned to the mine eight years later and, again, conducted interviews and observations, when Coal Co-operative was ten years old. I kept in contact with the mine during the intervening years between the visits. Three years later, the mine closed.

The alias "Valley Colliery" refers to the mine when it was nationalized and owned by the British Coal Board, while "Coal Co-operative" refers to the mine once it became a worker co-operative. This mine, located in Wales, was the last deep-pit in Wales and one of the few left in the United Kingdom. As such, employment at the mine—when it was still part of British Coal and after it became a worker co-operative—held important cultural significance for the miners, who were deeply identified with their occupation. During the period between the closing of the mine by the Coal Board and its reopening as a co-operative, some out-of-work miners took factory jobs, the only other jobs in the area. They described those jobs with much contempt, often saying that they would rather go on government assistance than work there again. Once the mine was reopened as a co-operative, workers had to become members before they could begin work at the mine. In order to participate, each worker had to buy a single share of the co-operative at £8,000 (approximately $13,000). As with the other two co-operatives, this share entitled the member to profit sharing as well as wages. When the worker left the co-op, the company would buy back the share.

Two Taxicab Companies

Both the conventional taxicab company (Private Taxi) and the co-operative taxicab company (Co-op Cab) are located in the same Midwestern city, which I call Prairieville. More than 30 years ago, striking cab drivers started Co-op Cab as an alternative to two of the city's main taxicab companies. Prairieville is the location for a Big Ten university town, well known for its progressive politics; both cab companies had reputations for employing overly educated drivers, often with advanced degrees (Langway 1997).

Co-op Cab embraced the worker co-operative ideology to try to create a better workplace, although not as uniformly or dogmatically as Organix Co-op. Workers at Co-op Cab became members once they had successfully completed a probationary period as determined by the membership committee. Once members, they shared in the profits of the company in addition to their wages.

My first visit to study Private Taxi was in 1998. I returned two years later, in 2000. Both times, I interviewed present and past workers and managers as well as made observations of the employees and supervisors at work. I first visited Co-op Cab the year of its 20-year anniversary, interviewing current and former members and conducting observations. I returned the following year, and again five years later. Co-op Cab is still going strong today.

The Organics Industry

I examined two organic food distributors: Organix Co-op, a worker co-operative located in the mid-north of England, and HealthBite, a conventional business located near London. Both companies distributed organic food; they did not produce any of their products. While some workers in the industry described the attraction of these jobs as simply providing a paycheck, others spoke of their dedication to the organic and whole food movement and saw the jobs as a type of activism.

Organix Co-op was formed more than 30 years ago by progressive college students who wanted to create a better, healthier, more egalitarian work environment. This spirited idealism still permeated the business. Workers at Organix Co-op became members after completing a probationary period and being voted into membership by the current members. Once they became members, they received their part of the company's profits, as well as wages; they became "vested" in the company, with each worker owning a single share of stock, regardless of tenure. When they left the co-operative, they would have to sell their share back to the company, generating a type of severance pay. I visited Organix Co-op twice, once in 1996 and again in 1997. Both times I interviewed members, probationary members, former members, and worker-managers. Organix Co-op is still a thriving business; however, it has changed its location to a small town in West Yorkshire.

I selected HealthBite Distributors for this study because it was similar to Organix Co-op in many ways, including the gender and racial balance of its workforce, the hours of the business, and the business's focus. HealthBite was formed when two individually owned organics wholesale businesses merged in the early 1990s. At the time of the study, HealthBite was primarily a distribution company, although individuals could buy merchandise at the warehouse. Two owners share the management of the business in the new London location. I visited HealthBite twice, once in 1996 and again in 1997, interviewing workers and managers and making observations.

Methods

One of the key benefits of qualitative studies is the high validity possible: the researcher can understand the greater context, obtain a large overview, and can triangulate the accounts of differently situated interviewees with various bases of knowledge. I employed a qualitative comparative case method (Ragin 1987) to study three very different industries, each with one co-operative and one conventional organization. In gathering data for this study, I interviewed workers; observed behavior; read related documents and articles; attended companies' business meetings and, when possible, grievance hearings; and participated in aspects of some businesses. (For example, I went down into the coal pit and rode along in the taxicabs.)

The interviews ranged from 20 minutes to more than five hours, with most lasting between 30 and 90 minutes. At least one especially lengthy interview occurred at each business. The main focus of the interviews was how the interviewee would handle potentially grievable circumstances. I asked general, open-ended questions, but with some direct questions, especially as follow-up inquiries. In discussing dispute resolution strategies, respondents often drew on examples from their past experiences.

All interviews and most site observations were tape-recorded and transcribed. The quotations included in this book have been edited for confidentiality, brevity, and readability. Most of the quotations presented here appear without ellipses and with few diacritical marks in order to preserve the flow of the text. The substance and tone of interviewees' remarks have been maintained, while attempting to eliminate awkward constructions that are often unavoidable in interviewees' spontaneous responses.

These data were analyzed using the qualitative data software NUD*IST Vivo, often referred to only as NVivo. NUD*IST is the acronym of Nonnumerical, Unstructured Data: Indexing, Searching and Theorizing. NUD*IST Vivo is the most recent version of this software program from Sage.

Using NVivo, I began by coding the transcribed interviews for various themes. Some of these themes were responses to explicit questions ("In what ways is your job difficult?"). However, many others were extracted from the responses of interviewees to broader questions ("How would you describe your job?", "How would you recommend/criticize your job to another worker in the same industry?", "What would you change about your job if you could just snap your fingers and it would be different?"); others were follow-up questions to other responses. Thus, a portion of the codes were not the result of a direct question or set of questions, but were produced by careful analysis of interviewees' responses to various questions, as facilitated by using NVivo.

The many benefits of using computer-assisted qualitative data analysis software include greater speed in coding and analysis, more complex ways of studying relationships in the data, text searches, and formal structure for developing analysis (Barry 1998). I used NVivo for cross-case analysis, to gather data together and explore them, and to reorder the hierarchy of codes. Discussions of dispute resolution at other jobs were labeled with "disputes," with one or more sub-categories, as well as with the category "other jobs." This allowed me to extract discussions involving only disputes at present jobs and yet also have the option of including reports of past grievance behavior at earlier jobs. The category "other jobs" was also used for any discussion of other positions the interviewee had held; it was used alone, such as for simple descriptions of other jobs, or with other categories, such as with "management" or "gender," for contrasts on specific aspects with the previous workplaces.

I began by coding on basic concepts: disputes, workplace culture, bad, good, and so on: I then "coded on," refining those codings into more specific sub-categories. For example, text coded as "disputes" was broken down into "formal," "informal," "procedures," "legal consciousness," "lumping," and "whining." Some passages of interview text received more than one sub-category. These sub-categories were further refined; sometimes I broke them down into even smaller categories and, other times I merged two or more categories. For example, I later collapsed "lumping" and "whining" into one category "toleration" that included both stoic acceptance and vociferous whining; both involved acknowledging a problem but taking no action to resolve it. Thus, the category of "toleration" is different from simply "silence" in that "toleration" encompasses both the unhappy, truly silent employee and the less-quiet employee who simply refuses to take an action to resolve the grievance.

Using NVivo's attribute function, I assigned attributes to each interviewee based on her or his company, industry, co-operative/non-cooperative status, and gender. Using NVivo's matrix and search functions, I compared responses from interviewees within and between companies, industries, and organizational structures. I contrasted their various responses regarding job involvement, dispute resolution, workplace power, gender dynamics, ideological commitment, and workplace socializing. NVivo also can generate tabulations of the number of occurrences of any coded item. For example, it can produce a chart showing how many interviewees at each business mentioned addressing disputes through formal means, informal means, toleration, or exit. The reader should note that these tabulations are not generalizable in any way. These tabulations are not from a quantitative random sample, but are descriptive statistics, illustrative of the balance of qualitative evidence.

Methodology

My primary data were collected through interviews, as mentioned above. Interviews are well suited to explore aspects of individual lives. As Collins rhetorically asks, "[W]ho better to ask than the individuals themselves?" (Collins 1998: 1.4). Other methods, such as participant observation and surveys are, respectively, difficult when studying a variety of places, as I did, or do not provide the level of detail and insight I sought (Collins 1998). A possible methodological weakness of interviewing is that interviewees might provide only the "official account," a reporting of what they feel ought to happen rather than what did happen (Bourdieu 1977). I addressed this directly in my interviews by asking questions about what should be done and what others would do, in addition to asking what the interviewees themselves would do. This provided the interviewees with opportunities to report the "official accounts" as well as any possible contrasts to their own expected behavior.

When I asked subjects how they would handle potentially grievable circumstances, some drew on past actions, while others only spoke of anticipated future action. Thus, the various dispute resolution strategies discussed in the preceding chapters refer to either anticipated future behavior or reported past behavior by interviewees.

In conducting the interviews for this project, I was aware that the traditional model of an interview was one of inequality, with the interviewer possessing greater power—and the gathering of information more valued than the providing of insights (Oakley 1981). However, I believe my interviewees had power. They were the ones answering, which I believe places them in a vastly more important—hence more powerful—role. They knew something I didn't, and knew something I wanted to know, which granted them some amount of power.

The power held by the interviewees was not usually abused, although some interviewees did exercise their privilege through good-natured teasing. For example, in one interview with a miner I used the term, "chairperson."

"Chairperson? ChairPERSON?!" he said, with, possibly mock, rage. "ChairMAN! Chairman." I apologized and said, "Good point. Wayne's a man; I'll say chairman."

Throughout the remainder of the interview he would emphasize the word "man" in "chairman" whenever he used the word again. Thus, there were many instances when the "masculine paradigm" of the interview (Oakley 1981: 38) did not seem to provide a distinct interviewer-interviewee hierarchy with me holding the power.

Additionally, the power I had because of my status as the interviewer was balanced by my status as a woman, as a shorter person, and as a younger person (younger than many of those I interviewed). At some sites, my status as an outsider and as an American sometimes provided me with more power, and at other times decreased my level of power. My status as a university student also cut both ways.

However, importantly, I had the power of agenda-setting (Gaventa 1980; Lukes 1974). I posed the questions, and, even if the interviewee refused to answer (which was extremely rare), the question remained asked. This power often compensated for my lesser power because of my age, gender, and lack of the interviewee's experiences and knowledge. For example, it would be inappropriate for a young woman to ask a man she recently met in a professional situation about how he schedules defecating at work. In this research, however, the level of autonomy at work was an important issue as it related to workplace grievances. In mining, being allowed to take breaks when one wanted—in particular, in order to defecate according to one's own schedule in a secluded part of the mine—was a key point of conflict between workers and managers at Valley Colliery. For this reason, I believed it was appropriate and even necessary for me to ask about this otherwise unmentionable topic. While this might have caused surprise, the interviewees answered the question directly. The power of being the interviewer not only allowed me to ask this, but created an atmosphere where the interviewee felt that it was acceptable to answer honestly. I had additional power because, as the researcher, I was not only the interviewer but also the narrator of the resulting story. While I did try to allow multiple voices to come through, ultimately, I had a great deal of power in how I told the story and, to a lesser degree, which subplots I emphasized (Atkinson and Hammersley 1994).

Throughout the data-gathering phase, I did, however, try to resist the "model interview" (Oakley 1981) with its aggressive grilling and obvious demonstrations of the interviewer's power. Instead, I tried to be engaged with the interviewees. Collins asserts that "engagement implies a willingness on the part of the interviewer to understand the interviewee's response to a question or prompt in the wider context of the interview(s) as a whole." (Collins: 1.6).

I also actively tried to share power by offering (brief) information of my own. These self-disclosures were usually in reaction to information just shared by the interviewee. For example, interviewees would talk about visiting places in the United States, and I would explain where I am from, usually in relation to Chicago or Dallas. One person mentioned playing the trumpet; I told him that my dad played the trumpet. One person talked about the difficulties of doing her job as a short woman. I described how the women in my family are all short and described our different ways of adapting to a tall world. As Collins has said:

> As the interviewer I am not, I cannot be, merely a passive observer in all this, even though it is primarily the interviewee's life which is under scrutiny. In encouraging the interviewee to tell me these stories and in asking them to develop a sub-plot here and a character there, I am encouraging them to construct and reconstruct themselves and [I] contribute to this by exchanging stories of my own. (1998: 3:10)

In other words, there is "no intimacy without reciprocity" (Oakley 1981: 51).

While I did engage in sharing a bit of my own stories during interviews, I did not share my most important story: my hypotheses, thoughts, and early analysis of this study. I also commented on more tangential remarks by interviewees, rarely speaking my own thoughts about the main focus of the study: discussions of workplace norms, disputing and grievances, gender dynamics, or co-operative or company philosophies. For these topics, I refrained from sharing because such comments could affect the substance of what the interviewees said on these subjects, thus tainting or even ruining the data I was trying to collect.

I was also extremely selective about sharing my emotions in interviews. First, I tried never to show negative emotions, such as disapproval, repulsion, or disbelief. I also faced complicated decisions regarding how to share my emotional reactions to interviewees' emotions. I did not believe that I could ignore them: "The emotions experienced, whether by interviewer or interviewee, are as real, as important, and as interesting as any other product of the interview. To ignore or discount manifestations of emotion is as unreasonable as ignoring the talk that objectivity demands we record" (Collins 1998: 3.35). However, I struggled with how much of my own emotions to show in response to their emotions.

Although I don't believe most interviewers can remain completely detached or fail to exhibit biased feedback, I did make an attempt to stay composed and present myself in similar ways at each interview, making my own reactions as unnoticeable as possible. Sometimes this was difficult. For example, several worker-managers at different co-operatives spoke, with much despair, about how they were seen in their new quasi-managerial roles. They told me that many people now saw them as turncoats or sell-outs, but, they insisted to me, they were still the same people, still working for the good of the co-operative and its members. In each case, I didn't even allow myself to nod, even though I agreed with their assessment of their situations.

Other times, I believed that *not* sharing my own emotions would have negatively affected the interview as much as sharing would have in the situations described above. This was particularly true when interviewees discussed extremely painful topics. Since the nature of this research was disputes and problems in the workplace, a portion of each interview addressed negative aspects of people's work lives. Sometimes, these discussions became quite emotional for the interviewees and quite affected me as the interviewer (such as when a homecare worker described the death of a client or a whole foods worker described harassment at a previous job so abhorrent that she quit). In these cases, I believed that I would have communicated a lack of understanding if I did not show at least a portion of my reaction—not only to the stories but also to the person's present pain—which they had to relive in order to tell me about it.

I believe that not only did I gain valuable data and experience through the interviews, but the interviewees benefited from the interview process as well. Many qualitative researchers mention that their interviewees benefit simply from being listened to, from being given the researcher's undivided attention: for example, Collins discusses becoming "a sympathetic ear" and providing interviewees with the opportunity to talk about topics they might not be able to discuss with people closer to them (Collins 1998: 3:31). Becker asserts that people with "disrupted lives" create meaning and order in their lives by talking about their lives with another person, such as a researcher (Becker 1997). In other cases, the researcher is asked (implicitly or explicitly) to act as the interviewees' confessor as they describe past actions they regret (e.g., Rubin 1992).

I believe my interviewees benefited from the opportunity to share their experiences with someone who listened, took them seriously, and validated them by including them in scholarly research. They also responded to my invitation to explore aspects of their lives on which they otherwise might not have reflected. Some interviewees said that they had never thought about some of the questions I asked them and said they enjoyed that self-exploration. Some commented that the interviews were "like therapy" in that they helped them explore themselves and gain new insights.

Works Cited

Atkinson, P. and Hammersley, M. (1994). *Ethnography and Participant Observation.* pp. 248–261 in Handbook of Qualitative Research, edited by N.K. Denzin and Y.S. Lincoln. Thousand Oaks, C.A.: Sage Publications.

Barry, C.A. (1998). Choosing Qualitative Data Analysis Software: Atlas/ti and Nudist Compared. *Sociological Research Online* 3.

Becker, G. (1997). *Disrupted Lives.* Berkeley: University of California Press.

Bourdieu, P. (1977). *Outline of a theory of practice,* edited by T.B.R. Nice. Cambridge: Cambridge University Press.

Collins, P. (1998). Negotiating Selves: Reflections on 'Unstructured' Interviewing. *Sociological Research Online* 3.

Gaventa, J. (1980). *Power and Powerlessness*. Urbana, Illinois: University of Illinois Press.

Langway, L. (1997). The Best Cities for Women. *Ladies Home Journal*, pp. November, 199–204.

Lukes, S. (1974). *Power: A Radical View*, edited by A. Giddens. London: The Macmillan Press.

Oakley, A. (1981). Interviewing Women: A Contradiction in Terms. pp. 30–53 in *Doing Feminist Research*, edited by H. Roberts. London: Routledge.

Ragin, C.C. (1987). *The Comparative Method: Moving Beyond Qualitative and Quantitative Strategies*. Berkeley: University of California Press.

Rubin, L.B. (1992). *Worlds of Pain: Life in the Working-Class Family*. New York: BasicBooks.

Subject Index

Author Index

For Product Safety Concerns and Information please contact our EU
representative GPSR@taylorandfrancis.com
Taylor & Francis Verlag GmbH, Kaufingerstraße 24, 80331 München, Germany